Dear Mary –

Best Wishes,

Lori

THE
Publican's Wife
FROM MILKMAID TO BARMAID

LORI PATRICK

Copyright © 2015 Lori Patrick

This book is copyright. Apart from any fair dealing for the purpose of private study, research, criticism or review, as permitted under the Copyright Act, no part may be reproduced by any process without written permission. Enquiries should be addressed to the Publishers.

All rights reserved.

Published by:
Boolarong Press
655 Toohey Road
Salisbury Qld 4107
Australia
www.boolarongpress.com.au

National Library of Australia Cataloguing-in-Publication entry:
Creator: Patrick, Lori, author.
Title: The publican's wife : from milkmaid to barmaid /
                Lori Patrick.
ISBN: 9781925236132 (paperback)
Subjects: Patrick, Lori.
                Hotelkeepers--Queensland--Biography.
                Women--Queensland--Biography.
Dewey Number: 647.94092

Typeset in Euclid Pro 12pt.

Cover Design by Boolarong Press.

Printed and bound by Watson Ferguson & Company, Salisbury, Brisbane, Australia.

I dedicate this book to

JAMES BARRIE PATRICK.

Contents

Acknowledgements   vii

Prologue   ix

Chapter 1   Who are You Calling an April Fool?   1

Chapter 2   Life on the Farm   13

Chapter 3   The Best Things in Life are Free   31

Chapter 4   Didn't We Have a Lovely Time   45

Chapter 5   Holy Snight   53

Chapter 6   The Milk Maid   61

Chapter 7   Romance Blooms   67

Chapter 8   Tying the Knot   81

Chapter 9   Head West Young Man   91

Chapter 10   Back to the Big Smoke   111

Chapter 11   Home on the Range   117

Chapter 12   Faraway Places   127

Chapter 13   Kegs, Kids and Cattle Dogs   137

Chapter 14   Ever the Showman   153

Chapter 15   Bus Coming!   161

Chapter 16   King of the Road   169

Chapter 17   Outback Kids   **185**

Chapter 18   Surf's Up   **201**

Chapter 19   The Big Wet   **209**

Chapter 20   Who Wants to be a Millionaire?   **217**

Chapter 21   Our Worst Nightmare   **227**

Chapter 22   Sea Change   **233**

Chapter 23   Count Your Blessings   **245**

Chapter 24   The Red Suitcase   **255**

Chapter 25   My Home Among the Gum Trees   **261**

Glossary   **267**

Acknowledgements

I would like to thank the many kind people who have helped me to finally put my story to bed.

Thank you to Tina who spent many hours in her tireless pursuit as 'project manager', Deb who took on the job of helping me with the images, which was no easy task, and Bronte for her illustrations. Thanks also to Graeme Harding for his professional advice and Duncan, Harry and Steve Donovan for their encouragement. My sister Barbara Hunter also gave me unfailing support, encouragement and knowledge of family matters, for which I am entirely grateful. I would also like to thank my brother Rob, his wife Jan, and David and Gwen Roderick for offering their properties for research and imagery.

Thank you to Boolarong Press, including Dan Kelly, Lesley Synge and the very helpful support staff.

Prologue

The modern world is moving so fast that when my grandchildren reach middle age they may find it hard to credit how things were before the age of technology. With this in mind, I started to record the memories of my life for my children and grandchildren. As I progressed nostalgia took over and I found myself reliving my very happy childhood and interesting adult life.

The fresh fragrances from the farm I grew up on, the aromas of many old houses we rented, the fresh ocean breezes from our holidays at Noosa, even the sharp stench of gidgee bugs as I cleaned up after a big night of entertaining tourists and truckies at the old Blue Heeler Hotel are just some of the senses I recollected as I worked on these reminiscences.

I relived the emotions too. I remembered the adversities Barrie and I faced during our nearly 50 years of marriage, along with the many glorious times we experienced. The chief blessing of our lives is our four wonderful children and now, in later years, our beautiful grandchildren. Although this is my story, for nearly 50 years of married life Barrie and I were a team. He was a somewhat colourful character and certainly livened up every experience we had and figures largely in my memories.

I also recalled many of the huge number of people who have crossed my path. Many were – and still are – close friends. It was impossible to do justice to the times we have shared in one short book. You know who you are; I thank each of you for so blessing my life.

Writing my memoirs has prompted me to reflect on the outstanding job my parents did in raising a big family in often difficult times. They were not wealthy, but nevertheless they brought plenty of riches to us children. This is not a family history, a diary, or an exact chronological description. It is a memoir, and the memories that underpin memoirs are funny things. I ask your indulgence because sometimes my recollection of an event or occasion will differ from that of a sibling or friend. Dad called his book *My Life As I Saw It* and that holds true for my book too – here is my life through my eyes.

The painter Margaret Olley once said that she lived in her painting ... gets lost in it, immersed in it. That's how I felt when I was writing. I hope you enjoy reading this book as much as I have enjoyed writing it.

CHAPTER 1

Who are You Calling an April Fool?

"Welcome to the Blue Heeler. Come on in – we won't laugh at ya. The Old Mare will play a few songs on the squeezebox for a sing-along and we'll take the pot around for the Flying Doctor. Throw in a few bob when we do." Barrie never completely converted to dollars and cents. He continued, "You never know when you might need the Doc on yer travels through the back-country".

These were the words that greeted many a busload of tourists when they arrived at our pub, the Blue Heeler Hotel, in Kynuna, outback Queensland. Barrie referred to me as the "Old Mare" to get a laugh. I'd then play "The Old Grey Mare Ain't What She Used to Be" and the tourists happily joined in. Never in my wildest dreams – at least for the first 30 years of my life – had I imagined owning and living in a *pub*! I'd had a very proper upbringing and it would have been taboo.

I was born on April 1, 1935 to Jessie Frances (nee Hollywood) and Walter Radford Harsant. Jessie and Radford lived on a 350-acre farm at Radford, near Harrisville in the

Fassifern Valley, about 25 miles from Ipswich. The old home is perched on a hill and overlooks the mountain ranges in the distance – Cunningham's and Spicer's Gaps to the south, Mt Flinders to the east and Mt Walker to the west. A lovely view whichever way you look, with the picturesque Warrill Creek bordering the farm. My brother, Rob, still lives on and works the farm with his wife, Jan.

Mum was born "out West" in Longreach. Her father, James Hollywood, was a blacksmith on Wellshot Station south of Ilfracombe at the time of her birth. Dad was born in the old home at Radford in the Fassifern Valley.

Dad's father, Walter Harsant, came to the farm in the late 1870s from New Zealand with his father, John, mother, Mary, and sister, Ann. The farm was then called Mt Radford. John Harsant served on and off for 14 years in the Maori Wars, but Dad said the Maoris bore him no ill will. Dad's great-grandfather had migrated to New Zealand from Norfolk in 1853, the first European doctor to practice in that country. He brought with him a wife and nine children. Dad's mother, Margaret, was the daughter of Thomas and Ann Roderick. Ann was a granddaughter of a recalcitrant convict, Hall Parcell, who was transported on November 19, 1821. This makes me a descendant of a convict.

People easily remember my birthday because it's on April Fools' Day, but when I was young the date of my birth had drawbacks as well as the advantage of being unforgettable. Children can be cruel and I was often the target of jokes and insults. April 1 is also publicised as a convenient day for remembering to change your fire-alarm batteries. (Mine are always in good condition.) As the story goes, I was two weeks overdue and there were several false alarms. Dad had the 1927 Oldsmobile revving so often in a state of anticipation that on this particular day when he was working in the lucerne paddock and received a message that Mum "had to go", he ignored it. He dismissed it as an April Fools' Day trick. Eventually he was convinced that it was the real thing and duly took Mum to the

Oakdale Private Hospital in Ipswich in time for the arrival of me, Lorraine Elizabeth, known as Lori.

I am the fourth of the family. Margaret Veronica, Barbara Jean and Kathleen Mary preceded me and Mirabel Frances, Walter John (known as John), Ann Jennifer and Robin Cedric followed. I often wonder how my parents afforded a private hospital when money was so scarce, but if you owned land you had to pay for hospital treatment, even in the public hospitals. Grandfather Harsant complained that the system was unfair, as landowners often had little money to spare. Mum and Dad also had a housemaid to pay and a car to run. Around the age of 10, when I first became aware of the importance of money, Dad's share of the profit from his family's farming business was £12 pounds a month ($24). That was in 1945. There wasn't much waste in our household.

One of the first family stories to be remembered about me is the day that Mirabel and I were taken to the church to be baptised. Apparently I was nowhere to be found until someone thought to look under the church. There I was, playing happily in the dirt.

My first strong memory is of a visit to the dentist when I was three. Before leaving for Ipswich I had a bath in a tin tub on the side veranda and I remember thinking, "How important I am! Going to Ipswich with only Mum, Dad and baby Mirabel in the car!" In those days it was an all-dirt road and if it rained it became slippery and dangerously exciting. (Admittedly, we usually didn't venture far if it looked like rain, and if we did, Dad carried chains for the tyres to prevent bogging and skidding.)

In his wisdom, the dentist removed 10 teeth under anaesthetic (gas). Those teeth would have been saved today.

After the job was done, my dear parents bought me a one-penny rainbow ice-cream cone and a little brooch in the shape of a blue, red and white sailing boat. Mum nursed me all the way home in the car and Mirie lay on the front seat between Mum and Dad. No seatbelts or restraints were used in those days, but the sedate speed made the journey safe and there were few other motor cars on the roads to contend with.

In later years, visits to the dentist in Ipswich were always exciting. They were the only times we visited "town". After the dentist appointments, Dad would take us to a café and shout us a meal. Because of its rarity, eating out was a big deal. In those days, Greek cafés flourished but they have all but disappeared now, replaced by pubs selling counter meals.

I can't recall any road accidents when I was very young, but when I was about 12 years old and Dad was taking us to Peak Crossing to perform in a concert, a man going in the opposite direction on the wrong side of the road (straight from the pub I believe) slammed into the side of our car. Fortunately the damage was slight, cars being much sturdier in those days, and we continued on our journey. The worst impact was on my nerves – when I played my piano solo, my fingers shook as they moved on the keys.

Mum said I didn't start talking until I was four. It has been said that I haven't stopped since! My first school was at Radford, a walk of about a mile, which was considered well within the capabilities of a five-year-old. After all, when Dad was young, he walked four miles to his school at Milora.

Radford School had desks for 24 pupils, but I never saw that many children in it. My teacher, Miss Jane McEniery, was very strict, but for the times could be very motivating. Art, singing and nature studies were important subjects, but the 3Rs were considered essential. Miss Mac was strict about getting the grammar right, something that seems less important in schools these days. We cleaned our slates with a tree sprig from the garden dipped in a jar of water and dried them off with a "slate rag". We didn't write on paper until we had been at school for at least three years. Once we reached that elevated stage, copybooks were used to help us learn to write on paper. We learnt to write legibly and neatly, first with pencils and later with ink. There were no biros then. Inkwells sat in holes in our desks, their glass sauce-bottle stoppers keeping out dust and foreign objects. Ink was made on site by mixing ink powder and water. The boys did the bottling and sometimes they put a garden worm in the inkwell to cause an awful smell, just to annoy the girls.

Miss Mac's beautiful handwriting was displayed on big, dusty, wall-mounted blackboards that were cleaned with a hard, flat "duster".

I had my first kiss at Radford School with a classmate who will remain nameless. We were sitting on a veranda learning from a big chart when he kissed me. On another day a boy said, "Do you want to see what I've got?" Of course I said, "Yes". To my amazement, he pulled his trouser leg up and showed me his "willy". I hadn't seen one before. My first encounters with the opposite sex! It was just before the first boy of the family, Walter John, was born.

When I started school in 1940, World War II was under way. In case the Japanese Imperial Army mounted an air invasion, the school committee (of which Dad was secretary) and some of the kids dug a slit zigzag-configured trench in the schoolyard. The school also provided little bags containing cotton wool for earplugs to protect our hearing and corks to put between our teeth. We hung those bags around our necks and on a signal we went very calmly to the trenches and squatted down with our heads between our knees. Grandfather Harsant, whose house was only a couple of hundred yards from the school, was in charge of the signal, a school bell. When he rang it, usually without warning, we headed for the trench. Fortunately we never had the need for the real thing.

To assist the "war effort", we knitted khaki and navy-blue socks, bootees, scarves and balaclavas. I remember knitting bootees in four-ply wool, using the feather and fan pattern. Even the boys had to knit for the "war effort" – Miss Mac made sure of that. We were very productive. We also had sewing lessons and in these we created samplers, bloomers, embroidery and so on. Miss Mac was also a keen gardener and had the school surrounds looking a picture. With the help of the pupils of course.

My memories of World War II aren't vast. To some extent, our parents protected us from much exposure. With the technology of today, with everything on TV or social media as it happens, or minutes after, we would have seen the war in a different light and been more aware.

I do remember the planes from Amberley Airbase practising over our farm, diving and performing mock battles. Convoys of army trucks and jeeps travelled along the main road only a couple of miles from our house, most impressive to a young girl. A lot of them were American, which made it even more interesting. If we needed to make a trip to Ipswich, we had to cross the runway at Amberley and often had to wait until the gates were opened after a plane had taken off or landed. The American Forces had big nights of R & R in the Harrisville School of Arts and stories abounded of how much good food they threw away. We heard stories of whole chickens, hams, bins of ice-cream – all the stuff we would have dearly loved to eat. We were envious.

There were two routes to school available to us: the long way by the road or the short cut through the McInnes's farm. The short cut was my favourite. Dad kept a track cleared through the long grass with his horse-drawn mower and pretty bluebells grew along its sides. After school we picked them for Grandma McInnes. She was Scottish and we thought the bluebells of Scotland appropriate flowers for the dear old lady. She always sat in a big lounge chair in her bedroom, knitting. Lovely pink and white periwinkles grew outside her room. She gave us lessons on turning the heel of a sock and sometimes treated us to boiled lollies.

Miss Mac was Roman Catholic and didn't take religious instruction classes, possibly because we were all "Proddos". Grandma McInnes's daughter-in-law, Mrs Sandy McInnes, came down the hill to teach us Protestants Sunday School in our school building. I signed the "Pledge" before I turned 10. I didn't think there would *ever* be a time when I would turn to "the demon drink". I have to admit the main attraction of taking the Pledge at the time was the possibility of getting a beautiful card with a blue wren on the front. I had never seen such beauty! Mrs McInnes had no trouble getting us to sign.

Four families were the mainstays of the school: us, the Harsants, the Parcells, the McFarlanes and the Turners. The three Parcell boys were "a bit rough", as could be expected of boys, and threw their weight around a bit at school, especially at soccer. One of them, Gary Parcell, went on to play Rugby League for Australia. One day on walking to school with the Parcell lads they kept yelling out, "Heil Hitler – the cow is dead". I thought they must have had a cow called Hitler, but at home that night it was explained that the dreadful Nazi we were fighting had at last met his end.

It might have been around this time that a dance was held in our large sleep-out with its polished floor and piano. The school supplied big white china cups for the supper and we kids helped Ken McFarlane to collect them in his jalopy. On the way home we had a flat tyre. Mr McFarlane mustn't have had a spare so he had us all out gathering long grass to stuff it with. We got to our destination without further trouble. In those days, you had to "make do".

By the time I was 10, Mirie, John and I were the only students left in the Radford School. Miss Mac was transferred to Ebenezer, the school closed and we three Harsants went off to Dad's old school at Milora, joining our sister, Kath, who was already there doing her scholarship year. Dad offered to drive Miss Mac to Ebenezer in his Oldsmobile ute. The Olds, purchased in 1927 and kept safely under the house, was once a tourer. During the war it'd been cut down to make it a ute. This enabled us to get extra petrol-ration tickets. We weren't allowed to sit on the side benches of the ute because the bumpy roads made it too hazardous, so we sat on the floor under a canopy to keep us a bit cooler. It was quite an adventure going any distance in the ute. Imagine the hard ride on the tray with no cushioning! If not getting around in the back of the Olds, we went everywhere by horse and cart or on horseback.

Horses were a very important aspect of our lives. A spring cart and slide, a wooden structure pulled by horses, was used to transport the cream to the road or the railway station on some farms. When we started at our new school at Milora we had to ride there. Kath and Mirie rode their own horses and I took young John until he mastered the art of riding. At that stage in 1945, we were aged 12, 10, 8 and 5, with Kath nearing her last primary-school years. Rob was born that year. By the time he and the other younger ones had to go to school it was to Harrisville State School by "bus". That sounds grander than it was – the "bus" was only a utility with a canopy!

We older kids had fun and games riding our horses to and from the Milora school. We raced, jumped logs and rode down steep gullies. On the way, others on horseback joined us. It was a four-mile ride, but first we had plenty to do before we set off. We had to get the 20 or so working and riding horses yarded and caught, and we rode bareback from the yards at the bottom shed up to the house to saddle up. The milking and separating of cream was also done. Following the milking we fed calves and pigs, and sometimes we even had to mind the milking cows grazing in the lucerne paddock. All this before breakfast and the ride to school.

The school had a large paddock for the horses. The saddles and bridles were kept in the play shed on its dirt floor, resting against the seats around the perimeter. I don't remember much play in the play shed. We passed our free time under a huge elm tree or under the school, which was built, Queensland-style, on tall posts. By early afternoon the horses gathered near the gate at the top of the paddock, eager to get home for a feed of hay. They wanted to bolt home, as horses do. It taught us horsemanship very young.

We were expected to be tough back then. I didn't wear shoes to school until I hit 12. Rain, hail or shine, we weren't allowed a day off. Once I had a huge carbuncle on the inside of my knee, most painful, but Mum made me saddle up and head off. Another day, having had to mind the cows on the lucerne, I was running late. The others left the gate open for me and my horse, Mildred, was so impatient to catch up with them she bolted through the narrow space. My leg caught on the barbed wire around the gate post. Nasty! I was taken to the Harrisville Hospital and Matron Pforr stitched the gouge up. The next day it was taken for granted that I'd saddle up and go off to school again.

Dad was often called upon to take some child or other from the farm into Matron for stitches. It was not always us Harsant kids, because sometimes the workingmen's children were injured. "They usually pick a wet day when the roads are slippery," he joked. Sometimes, injuries were not serious enough to warrant Matron. We used the ointments and medicines sold to us by the travelling salesman from Rawleighs. "Goanna Salve" was popular and very handy for people without easy access to town.

We acquired the art of horse riding early. I can't remember specific lessons but we were taught to ride by Dad or Grandfather, who led us around the farm on a lead rein when we were "knee-height to a grasshopper". We were then let loose solo in what we called "The Orchard" at the back of the house.

The grandly named Orchard was a fenced half-acre filled with fruit trees. The night horse for bringing in the cows night and morning for milking grazed there. Its hay and chaff was kept in a garage-sized tin shed adjacent to it. The tin shed contained the bridle and saddle for the night horse, the tack for our school horses and an old buggy used before the advent of the car. We kids loved to play in the buggy, travelling for miles in our imagination.

Dad taught us the intricacies of the harness and equipment for draught horses too: how to roll up the long reins, put away the collars and hames, how to detach the swingle tree chains and all the other jobs to do with working horses. We kept the working-horse harness in the bottom shed. A good-sized waterhole was nearby. We caught mullet, catfish and eels there. We'd ride the draught horses through the water to stir up the mud and when the fish leapt out, in fright I suppose or perhaps to gasp for oxygen, the workmen caught them with wire netting or hay forks. A feed of fish was always appreciated, a nice change of diet, even if they tasted a bit muddy.

When I was about 11 or 12, our friend Jimmy McGregor-Lowndes gave us a horse that stood at 16½ hands. Jimmy originally bought Cobra as a show hack, but when the novelty wore off, sent him up to us at the farm. Prior to his life as a show horse, Cobra belonged to the Queensland Police Force. He was a magnificent animal – and had the best credentials of any nag we ever owned. I was given Cobra to ride to school and for mustering. When I rode him in the Best School Pony Competition at the Milora School Diamond Jubilee, people simply didn't believe he was a "school horse".

Cobra was familiar with a curbed bit and martingale so we used these for a long time. Sometimes Mum turned up the radio music or played the pianola and I rode Cobra up to the open window. When he heard the music he danced sideways, remembering his training in the Police Force. I entered him in some competitions run by the Warrill View Annual Show.

One year I remember riding our horse Jimmy to pace the trotting horses competing at the Show. To prepare us for the horse events at the show, we took lessons on show-ring etiquette from Jim Burnett, a local gentleman. His lessons must have paid off because one year Kath competed at the Brisbane Exhibition, a major achievement for a horsewoman. We also competed in pushbike races on worn-out old bikes around the trotting ring. Shows were indeed great fun.

Another visitor to the farm in those days was Paddy Reddy, a well-known local. He came occasionally with his big stallion and when they arrived we kids were shuffled off to the house. We wondered what mysterious things were going on. Of course the stallion had come to service some of our mares to increase our horse stocks. During the war we sold some horses to the Indian Army, I believe.

Dad also rode Cobra. When Dad got older, he led Cobra up to where we had once started to build a tennis court. It had a graded section about 18 inches higher than the proposed court surface and made an excellent mounting block. In his old age arthritis plagued Dad, but he kept riding until he was about 80 years old.

Margaret, Barbara, Kathleen and baby Lori.

Lori on the front steps of the family home on the farm.

CHAPTER 2

Life on the Farm

My parents were wonderful people and I have very fond memories of them. Of course they were strict, particularly Mum, but they gave us all we needed and worked hard to give us kids a beaut upbringing. Some people kept the "strap" hanging on their kitchen wall as a threat of punishment to their children for misbehaviour – our kitchen didn't have one.

Keeping the household running was Mum's full-time job. It took her one and a half days to do the weekly wash. When a washing machine was eventually procured, a Pope model I think, it took her only one and a half hours! Before then we had a hand-driven mangle, or wringer, a contraption guaranteed to improve the arm muscles. Imagine the number of sheets and towels required for a large family! We always put the top sheet to the bottom and the bottom sheet was washed weekly – no fitted sheets in those days. Once when Mum was in hospital with a new baby, Dad told me he slept on one side of the bed for a week and then changed to the other side for the next week. "Got a fortnight out of a pair of sheets," he said proudly. By the time the first washing machine arrived a number of the daughters had left home.

We didn't change our clothes as often as you change your mind, as is often the case these days, so the personal clothing was nothing like the load a mother has to wash today. We didn't own too many changes, anyway. But mosquito nets, valances (the adornment on the mosquito-net frame, not the skirt around the mattress as they are today), pillow shams and doilies for the dressing tables and furniture went in the wash. The doilies were always starched. We didn't have spray-on starch then. Hills hoists hadn't been invented when I was a child so we had long clotheslines between two posts, with clothes-props holding up the lines in the middle. We had four lines like that. Mum didn't iron pillowcases or night attire as she said you ironed out all the fresh air. Folding sheets (a child at each end) was an after-school chore.

The wash tubs were under the kitchen of our high house on a long bench, which was also used for sorting clothes. Mum didn't have the luxury of a cement floor; it was packed earth, with a duckboard in case of spilt water. Dad used the laundry tubs to wash the dust of the farm off himself and clean his teeth. For dental care we kids leant over the back veranda railings with a cup of water, often using salt or charcoal instead of toothpaste. Dad's shaving arrangement was a source of interest. He would take a little drawer from the kitchen dresser to the kitchen table and sit down. All the shaving gear was kept in that draw. He sharpened his razor blade by rubbing the razor back and forth in a drinking glass. Then the shaving could commence. Of even greater interest, that drawer housed a little model of a naked boy that Dad picked up in Belgium just after World War I. I think he said it was a copy of a statue in a city there, where the little boy had water coming out of part of his anatomy, which was the cause of our intrigue and amusement. Dad used a "cut-throat" razor in his early years of shaving, sharpened on a razor strop, and then advanced to the safety razor, then to the Bic and an electric one later in life. No more blade sharpening. There were no sinks or hand basins in my younger days and the shower was located under the tank-stand enclosed by corrugated iron. A tin dish served for washing faces and the dishes, with an upside-down galvanised-iron stump cap for a draining tray.

Before three modern cement tubs came to the farm, the clothes were washed in three big tin tubs on the laundry bench under the house. The soap, which Mum often made herself, especially during the war, was grated into the copper boiler, which bubbled away in the yard a few metres from the door of the laundry area. Clothes were boiled before being washed and double rinsed in the tubs. Washing powder hadn't yet reached the farm. One of the rinse waters was blue, obtained from the Blue Bag, a must at the time. The Blue Bag came in handy for dabbing on green ant and other insect bites as well. The wooden laundry trolley had slats and a draining catchment, where the excess water ran back into the boiler. We only had a couple of rainwater tanks so there was no water to waste. A copper stick was essential for handling the boiling water and clothing. Mum had to give up making the soap due to a severe rash on her hands, probably caused by caustic soda or something else in the ingredients. The bar soap was bought in fairly large lots and stored on the floor-bearers above head height under the house. It was thought that drying it out and making it hard lengthened the life of the soap and saved money. It would have been easier to grate too, I imagine.

Looking at photos from my early childhood reminds me of another of our mother's duties – cutting our hair. I was a teenager before I went to a "proper" hairdresser. Until then my straighter-than-sticks hair was cut in pudding-basin style.

All around the under-house area was fenced in with battens. When I was about 15 and learning to drive, Mum asked me to back the Pontiac out from under the house. I was nervous and turned the wheel in the wrong direction, afraid of getting the car too close to the clothes-boiler fire. Consequently, I hooked the front bumper bar around the gate post, leaving it quite out of shape. The bumper bar, that is. I was shaking like a leaf wondering what Dad would say. I didn't like upsetting him. Mum instructed me to drive down the paddock to an electricity pole. Under her direction she got me to drive back and forth, aiming the bumper bar at it. Miraculously, it worked. You couldn't see any remaining damage, but my conscience got the better of me and I told Dad later. As mentioned previously – cars were tough in those days. Luckily for me, Dad wasn't!

The stove recess was a popular place on a winter's morning while the porridge was cooking. Mum, being of Scottish descent, believed a breakfast of porridge would always get you through the morning. Rolled Oats or Breakfast Delight were her specialties! In the evenings Dad often wiped the dishes, letting us get on with our homework. I remember one night as we bent our heads under the light of a kerosene lamp that Barbara asked Dad for inspiration in writing a sentence using the phrase "fits and starts". Dad knew that Mr Browne, the headmaster at Milora School, had an old Whippet car of which he was extremely proud. Dad advised Barb to write: *The Whippet goes in fits and starts.* I don't know if Brownie was impressed.

Looking back, it was generous of Dad to help in the house at night after slaving on the farm from pre-dawn to dusk. He was a good husband and father. The Best. We had kind, loving parents, were always well fed with good food on the table and clean sheets on the beds.

As well as looking after a large and busy household our mother was a member of the Harrisville Queensland Country Women's Association (CWA). In fact she was a foundation member as was Grandma Margaret Harsant, her mother-in-law. If she wanted to go to meetings, or out to other activities, Mum had to learn to drive the Oldsmobile. She ended up teaching herself. One day she wanted to visit her sister in Harrisville. Dad said, "I don't have time to take you but if you can get the car out from under the house you can go". She said, "Don't worry, I often back the car out while you are down the farm". She managed it and off she set with a couple of littlies on the front seat with her. She had a bit of trouble negotiating the Carson's front gate, but she got the car back unscathed.

Prior to the car, she drove a horse-drawn sulky to CWA meetings. In later years she did quite a few long trips as the chief driver very competently.

Milking is the centre of any dairy farm, and our working lives revolved around the dairy, which was a long building facing north, with drainage downhill from the bails. The motor, vat and separator were in a separate part, but all under the same roof. After milking, we youngsters carried the five-gallon drums of separated milk down the hill to the pigsties to feed the pigs. The pigsties were situated there to keep them out of sight and to keep the odours away from the house. We also fed them molasses, which we liked to sample by dipping in a finger.

Our dairy had four bails, with two cows to a bail, one either side. A huge difference from today's milking arrangements, where herds of hundreds are common; the small dairies having folded. The workers now stand at the back of the cows at a lower level to change the cups. Milking machines were introduced at our place about 1920-21, with a Moffatt Virtue plant of four units, the only milking machine from Riverview to the Great Dividing Range. In 1925 the Harsant family was the biggest cream supplier to the Queensland Farmers Co-op in an area between Grantham, Laidley, Boonah and Booval. We still had the Moffatt Virtue machines when I became a "dairy maid" after I left school.

A fellow came to the farm looking for work one day and Dad showed him around the dairy. "Do you know how to operate this engine?" he asked, pointing to the diesel engine.

"Oh yes," said the fellow, "the old READ. Know it well." Actually, the words on the brass plate on the side of the engine were: *READ instructions carefully.* The motor was probably a Lister or Southern Cross. Nevertheless, Dad gave him the job and watched him carefully until he was sure he knew what he was doing. He was one of the many workers Dad remembered in his memoir he wrote at about 80. He listed 146 names of men he knew or "had heard of" who had worked on the property. He had a prodigious memory. Incidentally, many of Dad's mates called him Casey. We just knew him as "Dad".

After the introduction of electricity, Dad purchased a large fridge. The dairy refrigerator could hold 16 milk cans and took up the space of the equipment no longer needed, such as the engine and separator. Since we no longer separated the milk, we stopped keeping pigs and concentrated on milk production.

We had to chain the cow into her bail and sometimes tie back one leg with a rope to avoid being kicked. And it was not good if they kicked the bucket of milk out of your hand. If they were cranky, old cows or nervous, young ones they made quite a mess with their bodily functions too. If they dirtied in the bail there was always a shovel handy to get rid of the droppings. (It would be worse now with the milker standing behind the cow.) After the machine had done its work, one had to "strip" the udders into a bucket in case all the milk hadn't come away by machine, thus the need for the milking block. To let the cow out of the bail one had to manipulate an overhead long piece of wood from near where you sat to open the gate in front of the cow.

I remember when Mum wanted to have a Jersey cow, much to Dad's disgust, as there had never been a Jersey on the farm before. Mum won the argument, saying that the milk of the Jersey would give us creamier milk and better butter, which was just what we children deserved. The Jersey had to be milked by hand, to isolate her rich milk from that being processed by machine. When I was very young, the cream was taken to the railway at Radford by horse and spring cart.

During the War, or just after, the farm ceased its employment of the large numbers of men, which was common in the earlier days. Mechanisation, fewer men available for farm work, as well as the cost of labour, were major factors in the change of scene. Dad and Uncle Cedric were in half-shares on the farm. I reckon Dad should have received more of the income, as he supplied so much "child labour". Perhaps he did get a bigger share – but I doubt it. I was never appraised of such details.

After we bought the big fridge, trucks transported the dairy produce. The afternoon milk was stored in the fridge overnight to go on the truck in the morning with that morning's milk, all of which was snap chilled. We rarely used the separator after that, although the cream shed, a small building near the dairy, was occasionally used for storage when the milk could not be sent away when breakdowns occurred or floods prevented the truck from coming. If we had a power blackout, we milked our 50 odd cows by hand. I can still see Dad on the milking stool, head buried in the side of the cow's hide, staring "o'er the plain", as it were. When asked what he was looking at he would answer, "I have to look somewhere don't I?"

For a while after we started to refrigerate the milk, Mum used a small hand-driven separator to produce our own cream, which then had to be turned into butter with a butter churn screwed to the kitchen table. Making our own butter was always a chore. Barbara, the bookworm of the family, did a lot of churning, nearly always with her nose in a book.

After we were connected to the electricity, refrigeration made things much easier in the dairy. Harrisville was connected in May 1941, one of the first townships in the Fassifern area to be supplied. The Harrisville School didn't join the grid until 1950. I don't remember what year electricity was installed at home, but I remember the first day we had the power. Our relations, the Carsons, came out to visit from Harrisville. Mary Carson and Mum were sisters. We were all running about the house turning on lights until the parents chastised us for wasting power. "Switch it off!" is still an automatic reaction for me. Over the years, the electricity supply to the farm brought electric radios, washing machines, irons, floor polishers, vacuum cleaners, driers, microwave ovens and air-conditioners.

We were shareholders in the Booval Butter Factory, and after we stopped making our own butter Mum ordered it by the box from the factory. The milk truck brought it. There was plenty of room in the dairy fridge to store it. Although our farm no longer has a dairy, there are still some big dairies in the district that send their produce in large tankers for processing.

After electricity, the next most radical home improvement was the indoor bathroom and toilet. Some people of the era didn't like the idea of "doing it" in the house and went to great pains to have the new installation as far from the kitchen and dining area as possible. "It can't possibly be hygienic!" they said. Dad no longer had the odious weekly job of "emptying the lav", although he continued to use the old thunderbox until it eventually blew over in a storm.

There was no such thing as toilet paper, but newspaper, apple papers (fruit bought by the case was wrapped in tissue paper) and later old phone books were satisfactory. At our place, anyway. The newspaper was cut into handy squares and pushed on to a protruding nail on the wall of the loo. When I got older, I tried to modernise the toilet-roll holder by threading the paper on to a wire and attaching it to the nail. Mum called the toilet "The Dub", although I'm not sure why. (Maybe it was from her Scottish ancestry.) The contents of the back-yard thunderbox were buried weekly, or more often in our case, usually by the man of the house.

The Carsons in Harrisville had a "Sanitary Man" calling once a week to their farm. They had quite a few daughters and apparently the can overfilled on one occasion. The poor chap remarked to Uncle Bill, "It's runnin' down me back, Bill. The girls must be home". I still remember an old joke I first heard about 60 years ago. One of the sanitary trucks had turned over and a worker was looking for his coat under the cans. "Leave your coat," the boss said to him. "It won't be any good now." The worker replied, "I'm not worried about the coat – I want my lunch out of the pocket".

We had no problems with bites from the infamous redback spiders that frequented toilet seats, but one night, when she was greeting Uncle Bill and Aunty Mary Carson at the back door, one bit Mum on the chest. Uncle Bill happened to be smoking a pipe and he immediately pulled out some of its contents and placed them on the wound. Nicotine supposedly cured redback bites. We did encounter a snake in the lav a couple of times. It's a big shock when you are about to sit down and you see a snake coiled up on the lid.

With the installation of the new bathroom we could have a bath lying down, and with hot water to boot. At one stage we had a long, painted cement bath in the old bathroom under the tank stand, with only cold water available. The builders must have been long-suffering chaps, putting up with kids under their feet as we watched them working. During the major improvement of the indoor bathroom I developed a liking for carpentry and gathered up all the off-cuts of timber, Masonite and bent nails I could find. I straightened the nails and tried to make things like little tables. I even dabbled in fibro-cement, from which there was plenty of sawdust. So far none of us has been diagnosed with the awful disease caused by fibro, a much used product in "the old days". Perhaps we didn't get enough exposure at the time.

In early times Dad hired workers to help on the farm and Mum had help to cook for "working men" plus her large brood of children. The Laegal family supplied some household help as well as Ethel Greuer, who was being courted by a local farmhand, a big man named Tarzan. One night as he was riding home after a bit of romancing on our back steps his horse fell and broke its neck at the bottom of the hill near the front gate of the farm. Tarzan survived unhurt, but the horse died and they burned the carcass the next day.

One of our working men had eight children in eight years by which time their mother had turned 28. They travelled everywhere by horse and sulky. The parents and the youngest children rode in the sulky and the older kids trotted alongside. They were probably pretty fit. Junk food wasn't around in those days and I don't remember ever seeing any overweight kids when I was young.

That family lived in a cottage down on the flat, near the gully. A good-sized heap of rubbish, including jam and Camp Pie tins, sprang up near their abode. There were a few cut feet, and Dad had to take the injured kids off to Harrisville to see Matron Pforr for stitching more than once. After that family left, we found they had removed a floorboard from the veranda to use as a toilet. Saved them walking down the back yard.

One very staunch and loyal family we had working on the farm was Alec Brook and his wife, Hazel, and their children who lived in the cottage down near the gully. Dad counted Alec as one of his best mates. They were a very hard-working and honest family who did very well in later life. When I was little, I loved to stay with one particular working man and his wife in their cottage on the hill near the main home. It was only 50 yards from our house and, when the farm was purchased by the Harsants in the 19th century, had been the main residence. It was luxury to me, to visit and be spoilt by the Rossiters. In fact, Mum told me as I got older that I called myself "Orrie Ossiter". Another name I called myself was "Waine Widdidty" (my version of Lorraine Elizabeth). Apparently the Rossiters wanted to adopt me. I think they were lucky that my parents declined the offer. I was ignorant of this fact, but remember thinking that if I was a Rossiter I'd like to be called Jill, my favourite name. I certainly didn't know anyone of that name; perhaps I got it from the nursery rhyme Jack and Jill.

Once overnighting with another workingman and his wife, I heard Dad's name mentioned. "Little pigs have big ears" I then heard. I took it to mean that they were running either Mum or Dad down. We were always told to be seen and not heard – it didn't stop you listening though.

When the last-mentioned couple was leaving and shifting out of the cottage they wanted us kids to help catch their chooks to take with them. Mum must have been dirty on them for some reason because she refused to let us help, instead taking on the task of teaching us girls how to cook biscuits. We started off on jam drops, then patty cakes. Despite my best efforts, I never turned out to be as good a cook as my mother.

After-school chores included feeding the chooks, locking them up as the foxes were bad, and getting in the firewood and chopping chips for the morning kitchen fires.

Weekends were pretty busy for us too. Dad's brand was 9WH and sometimes we helped with the branding of the calves, and we regularly helped with the dipping. Cattle were dipped at

regular intervals to reduce the cattle-tick infestation. We drove
the dairy cows from the home farm, or the bullocks, breeders
and "dry" cows from the two grazing paddocks, Mahaffey's
and The Washpool (each a few miles from the farm), to the
dip, which wasn't far from the railway station. Sometimes we
split into two teams and did both paddocks on the same day,
or sometimes we shifted them from one paddock to the other.

When I was about 12, the lot just dipped wanted to head
back to their "old" paddock. I was riding Cobra when they
took off in the direction opposite to which I was supposed to be
driving them. I took off at full gallop to turn the lead cattle, did
a quick turn on a muddy road bordered by a barbed-wire fence
and Cobra fell with me under him. We eventually got untangled
and on the move again. I turned the mob just before we got to
the railway line. While the cattle moo-ed and Dad yelled, the
train carrying our cousins, the Carsons, arrived.

I headed back to Mahaffey's with my sisters and we
hurriedly put the cattle back in the paddock and headed for
home, five or six miles away. By this time I was feeling pretty
crook from the fall. My stomach felt sore and my knee hurt.
We had lunch and a bit of a game with my cousins, June and
Pomp Carson, and enjoyed a quick look at the comics they had
brought with them. I was genuinely crook from the fall and
suggested that I wasn't up to going back to the cattle work.
Mum had other ideas. "There's nothing wrong with you," she
said, thinking I was making excuses to stay home with my
cousins. Somehow I found the strength to do the job. A full
day's dipping would entail at least 20 miles of riding by the
time the cattle were mustered and driven to and from the dip
yards, but we were conditioned to it from an early age.

Over the years there were plenty of busters as we were
forever riding horses, but fortunately no-one was ever seriously
injured. Barbara's accident was perhaps the worst. She took a
tumble off a horse once, and as a result carried a dimple in one
cheek for the rest of her life.

Dad himself experienced plenty of accidents. The most memorable one involved dipping. When he was about nine he was pulled into the dip by a cow and dragged under by her back legs. They rescued him and sat him in a nearby dam, and rinsed him off. Surprisingly, he was OK. Arsenic didn't have a bad effect on him as he lived to 82.

We also did dehorning, branding and castrating at the dip yards. Most of our cattle were dairy stock, but male calves were kept to fatten up as bullocks for the meat trade, so had to be "cut". When he was castrating calves, Uncle Cedric liked to throw the testicles around, asking if anyone wanted a feed of steak. I realise now that this was out of character for Uncle Ced. Perhaps he became more "proper" after his later marriage.

An angry bull could put us up the rails or a mob of bullocks could charge us while we were drafting off the "fats". We often drove a consignment of seven or eight fat bullocks, each week in the season, to put on a rail wagon in Harrisville where there were holding yards and loading facilities. Radford only had a rail line with a little station building and a goods shed, so we couldn't load the cattle or produce there. The bullocks were destined for the Cannon Hill saleyards in Brisbane. It was a five-mile ride to Harrisville. "The Girls" had the responsibility of taking the cattle to the trucking yards, usually in the afternoons after riding the four miles back from school. When we were older, Margaret brought her city fiancé, Keith Trail, to the farm for a weekend and we took him with us to dip the cattle. A lovely fellow, Keith, and a bit of a larrikin, but inexperienced where horses were concerned. When we asked him to block the cattle from running up a certain lane, he decided he was better off on foot, shooing them with his hat in hand.

Sometimes when we were older, we rounded up stray horses into the dip yards and a rodeo rider and friend, Ken Parrett, put on a rough-riding display – great fun with nothing else to do.

We were also involved in agricultural pursuits. "The Girls" drove the wagons of chaff and produce to the Wilsons Plains siding to put on rail to be sold at the markets in Brisbane. Kath was particularly deft at handling the horse teams. Once when she and I were helping with the chaff cutting, Britain, an old draught horse, was in the shafts of a dray near the ramp where we loaded the bags of chaff. Dad always told us to be careful of Britain's feet as he was known to kick, but I must have forgotten that advice as I fell from the front of the dray, right at his back feet. Kath nearly had a fit, but I managed to scramble out of his way in time, unharmed.

Eventually an old Bedford truck took over the carting of the hay, chaff and other produce from the horses. Then when baled hay became popular, our chaff cutting ceased. When we did cut chaff, lucerne or lucerne mixed with oats, Uncle Cedric fed the cutter (mind your hand), with the kids or a working man feeding him the hay. Dad sewed the bags as they filled, ready to transport to the rail at Wilsons Plains. It was a very dusty, noisy job, especially for Dad, with a diesel engine running the chaff-cutter. The dust and Dad's flannel shirts must have caused him some discomfort at times, because he scratched his back by rubbing it against a post or the wall.

On one occasion, Dad was driving horses with a high load of fresh lucerne hay into the shed. "Whoa," he said, but the horses didn't respond. His head came in contact with a large beam, knocking him off his feet. Shock, horror! We thought he was dead. But Dad was made of sterner stuff and was soon on his feet. I think his shins came in for more damage than most parts of him. "Always barking my bloody shins!!" he would complain. If we asked Dad if any of his injuries hurt, he'd say, "Only when I laugh". Another of Dad's favourite sayings was describing a nap: *five minutes with the Lord.*

Horses were used to mow, rake, harrow and roll the cultivation paddocks. I loved the evocative smell of newly mown hay, especially lucerne after we'd spent the day mowing and raking it. When it was left out in the paddock at night its aroma was delightful. As kids we helped with the "cocking" of the hay in the paddock – changing rows of mown lucerne into little "cocks" ready to be loaded on to the horse-drawn wagons and taken to be stored, sometimes in a haystack in the open, other times in the hayshed. Making a haystack was quite an art. Not that we girls attempted it. The wheaten and oaten hay was cut in the paddock and a machine formed it into sheaves. Our job was to stand these up on end, against each other, to dry out before being stored in the hayshed. This was called "stooking" and the machine was called a reaper and binder.

We Harsant girls were very handy, especially during the war when manpower was scarce and Uncle Cedric was away serving. Grandfather bought us a new tractor, a red Massey-Harris, in recognition of the girls' war-time effort, which made the work easier. (Didn't make the milking any easier though.)

We were rarely idle. If not working on the farm, Mum kept us busy around the house on a Saturday. Floors had to be polished regularly, down on our hands and knees, and the brass doorknobs received similar treatment. Wasn't Mum pleased to eventually get an electric polisher! Mum was good on the sewing machine, especially when making our bloomers and pyjamas. She also made the bedspreads for all the beds in the large sleep-out. She used unbleached calico edged with dark-blue cotton. I believe she worked for a tailor before she married.

Saturday was also the day that the yard had to be swept, chooks fed and chips chopped for the stove. It was also the day for a regular dose of senna leaves for health reasons (whether needed or not), and the occasional dose of castor oil. The theory that castor oil can have an adverse effect did not reach our household until many years later. We'd be playing around the old pepperina tree when Mum came out with the bottle and dosed us. Whenever I stand under that old tree now when visiting my brother, Rob, on the old farm, the memory of it rushes back at me.

The phone was a great innovation, especially in times of sickness, and later, when she had more time, Mum could have a good natter to the ladies of the district. When we had the telephone connected we supplied the tall poles for it – a big undertaking. The trees were cut down on Mahaffey's paddock and transported home on a horse-drawn "timber jinker". Mahaffey's paddock was a great source of products to meet our requirements – grass for grazing, ant-bed for the tennis court (that never eventuated) and trees for the telegraph poles. Dad was a jack-of-all-trades and of course it fell to him to drive the horses.

There were at least four harnessed together, playing up and rearing, and Dad was doing his block. He had a young horse in the team and it didn't want to cooperate. I was sure Dad would be killed before the end of the day, but much to my relief he turned up that afternoon triumphant and with the required poles on board. Dad was very versatile and the hardest jobs always came his way. He did a fair bit of work on a horse-pulled scoop for cleaning out dams and gullies when he was young, a very taxing job. Those jobs probably had a lot to do with him being the oldest male child in his family and with the biggest family of his own to support. When it came on the market, Dad wanted to buy Mahaffey's paddock from his sisters, but owing to a little "misunderstanding" was bypassed.

Our first phone was big and wall-mounted, with a fairly short lead. The mouthpiece was part of the instrument high up the wall, so one had to sit on a high stool to have a conversation of any length. I bet Mum was glad to convert to the newer, table model when they became available. We were on a "party line" with Grandfather Harsant. It was a shared line going to the exchange, and our number was 31U. Ours had a short-short-long ring and Grandfather, 31D, had a long-short-short tone. We children were not allowed to use the phone except in rare circumstances. (In our wildest dreams we wouldn't have imagined children in their early school days with mobile phones of their own.)

By 1946 the phone connection was up and running. A telephonist connected a caller to the number they wanted. A three-minute restriction applied to long-distance calls. The "switch girl" (I don't remember boys doing the job) would say,

"Three minutes, are you extending?", and she would give you another three minutes if required. Due to the cost most people didn't extend too often. Sometimes, if the telephone exchange was busy or the operator had to use the bathroom, you were lucky enough to get more than three minutes. (How would the modern young people manage today if they were restricted to three-minute calls?)

Despite the mod-cons we were starting to acquire, Mum must have been disillusioned at times. I remember seeing her take a hammer and remove the name plate we had on the front of the house, Callide, and throwing it down the hill. She said it hadn't brought any luck and she would get rid of it.

I think one phone-call contributed to this. In the middle of the night we heard the party line ring. It turned out to be a call about our young neighbor, Dorothy McInnes, who was pregnant at the time. She had to go to hospital. Of course, Mum and Dad were concerned about Grandfather's phone ringing at such an hour, and investigated as soon as possible. It turned out that Dorothy had contracted polio.

To my horror at around midday the next day I noticed that my younger sister, Ann, couldn't lift her left arm. She was feeling unwell and had stayed in bed. Being aware of the polio outbreak at the time, Mum was straight on the job and called an ambulance. The Brisbane General Hospital confirmed our worst fears – Ann had contracted the disease. Since I had slept with her the night before I was afraid that I would get polio too, but I was spared. To add to our woes, Dad was called away to Brisbane that morning to be with his mother, who was in hospital. It was a very traumatic time with the ambulance coming to the house for Ann – something we kids had never seen before.

Ann was four years and nine months when she contracted Poliomyelitis on May 26, 1946. It was formerly called Infantile Paralysis. Grandma Harsant died the same day. When Ann left the house in the ambulance I thought how unfair life was with our dearly loved grandma and our little sister both in hospital. I cried for hours. Grandfather Harsant died on 26th February the following year. It was said that the devastation caused to the farm and fences by a huge flood that year hastened his demise. It was a 12-month period of much upheaval, sadness and worry.

Ann spent many years in the Sylvia Moffatt Ward at the Brisbane General Hospital. When Ann and Dorothy McInnes succumbed, polio was rife on the Darling Downs, especially in boarding schools. A very nasty, dusty, westerly wind was blowing that week and I've always thought it blew the disease of polio in with it. It was a wonderful thing when a vaccine was found. I can't understand people who won't vaccinate their children. They clearly have never seen a bad epidemic.

Mum and Dad drove in the Olds to Brisbane every second Sunday to visit Ann. When our sister, Margaret, worked in Brisbane at the Commonwealth Bank she visited Ann on alternate weekends. Aunty Jean and Grandmother Hollywood also visited when possible. During the time Ann was in hospital, sailors from a visiting ship offered to help the nurses take the patients to the Brisbane Exhibition, which was in full swing across the road. The little ones were lucky that day.

After a few years in hospital, Ann went to live with Mum's sister and brother-in-law, Aunty Jean and Uncle George May, at Hardgrave Road, West End, Brisbane. The Mays had no children so it was a new experience for them and a boon to our parents to have their help. Ann could access physiotherapy as an outpatient from their place. Luckily, the Mays lived across the road from the West End School, which Ann attended.

Ann eventually came back to the farm and attended Harrisville State School. Polio never stopped Ann from living a normal, successful life and having a career. She worked for big corporations in Brisbane until her retirement, living independently in her own home. Ann is possessed of great character and despite a few setbacks in life has come out a winner with her courageous and positive attitude. I believe October 23rd is now a dedicated "World Polio Day". It is wonderful to know that the disease is almost eradicated, except in a few countries less advanced than ours.

Radford State School with siblings –
Barbara, Kathleen, Mirabel and John.

Lori riding to school on Cobra.

CHAPTER 3

The Best Things in Life are Free

Among a variety of crops we grew corn on the farm, most of which was sold by the corn-sack, but we saved some for feeding our chooks and ducks. A corn cracker, turned by hand, usually by one of "the kids", converted the corn into feed suitable for the farmyard avian population. (We did a lot of turning in our childhood days, what with the corn cracker, the cream separator, the butter churn and the meat mincer!) We grew potatoes and pumpkins and sat in the hayshed cutting the potatoes into planting-size pieces, making sure there was an eye or two in each piece. We'd cut up the best type of pumpkin, clean out the seeds to dry and keep them for planting during the next season. We also learnt the art of getting the most pumpkins possible into a bag to send to market. Dad was a genius at that.

Our produce was railed from Wilsons Plains to the Brisbane Markets at Roma Street. By the 1960s semi-trailers and large vehicles were causing too much congestion in the city and the markets shifted to the outer suburb of Rocklea.

The butcher called on a Friday with the weekly meat order, which always included a large piece of corned silverside or brisket, plenty of mince and sausages and often tripe. On weekend mornings we often had sausages, eggs, steak, mince or occasionally bacon for breakfast. We always had a roast dinner on the weekend. One of the offshoots of the roast-beef meals was bread and dripping, with salt and pepper – yummy! The grocer, fruiterer and baker also delivered to the house.

Sometimes we had chook or duck. We girls had to behead the sacrifices – one was not enough for our large family – with an axe on the chopping block at the woodheap. We then plucked and dressed the birds on the bench near the laundry tubs. This meant dipping each dead bird in boiling water, pulling out all the feathers and then dragging the innards out of it, discarding the gizzards and keeping edible parts, like the giblets.

I remember the last time I killed the chooks. I didn't sever one head properly and the poor old chook did back somersaults all around the woodheap. I couldn't stomach the job after that and said to Mum, "I won't do it any more. I'd rather get the strap". I hated that job and certainly couldn't do it now.

We bred a lot of ducks, which kept us fed for years. We started off with a duck and a drake and ended up with more than 100. Dad became very annoyed when they rested on the cool concrete floor of the dairy and left "duck brek" (as dad called the droppings) all over the place. We chased the ducks out at afternoon milking time and they waddled off to the house to be fed and locked up. Our chook and duck run was quite large and the eggs were laid all around, near the choko vines, mulberry trees and weeds, as well as in the henhouse. They had free run of the farm except at night. City kids holidaying with us loved collecting the eggs. Visiting city-ites also enjoyed fresh milk and cream straight from the dairy. One cousin made us laugh when she said that she'd always thought milk came from horses because a man with a horse and cart delivered the milk to them in Brisbane.

At times we had troublesome hawks stealing our eggs, little
chickens and ducks. Mum would get out the .22 rifle; she was
a good shot. Mum bought 100 one-day-old chickens at a time
and had them railed to the Radford Station. They were usually
white leghorns, although we also kept black hens and Rhode
Island reds. When they were small, we put the chickens in the
box they came in and stored it in the "lav" overnight. In the
morning we released them into their enclosure, usually a section
of an old rainwater tank. Our poultry, with the run of the farm,
was all free-range, so we were brought up on organic chooks and
eggs.

We had mulberry, fig, peach and loquat trees and Mum
made wonderful jam from the rosellas and wild gooseberries.
Sometimes we took a horse and cart a few miles to the bullock-
fattening paddock where there were three orange trees growing
on the creek bank. We backed the cart up under the trees, filled
it with oranges and headed for home with our booty. Other folk
in the district also used the trees for their citrus supply.

If you add oranges to the produce from the farm – pumpkins,
potatoes, beetroot, peas, beans, watermelons and rock melons,
plus the dairy products, and the cases of apples which came
on the train – we were nurtured on a pretty healthy diet. We
also ate a lot of chokos, usually served with white sauce. Some
people used them as pseudo pears, cooked with something to
sweeten them, to resemble tinned pears.

As we grew older we enjoyed the treat of a bottle of cordial
essence mixed with cups of dissolved sugar. This was our only
soft drink. When Mum made jelly, custard or a pie (as she did
most weekends), she put her cooking out on the tank stand near
the kitchen window to cool down. Luckily we lived in a high
house and the dogs couldn't reach the delicacies.

In the early days we kept food fresh in the "Coolgardie safe",
shortened by us to the "cool safe". It was a perforated metal
safe, with water in the top and cloth towels down the side that
the water seeped through to cool the contents – butter, cold
meat and other perishables. We really went modern when we

bought a kerosene fridge and loved the ice-blocks we could make with cordial or milk. The frequent weekend visitors from Brisbane loved going to the dairy and getting a jug of cream to go with the Gramma Pie, made from a sweetened pumpkin-like vegetable.

Mum was also a whiz at sponge cakes, and turned out some beauties if we had visitors for afternoon tea, especially on weekends when the Brisbanites visited. (Nothing like a weekend trip to "the farm".) At weekends we often had a big crowd at the dinner (lunch) table, and in those days, visitors or not, we all sat at the table for all our meals. You stayed at the table until everyone was finished, and until you had eaten all the food on your plate. One needed permission to leave the table before Mum and Dad. Table manners were important. We said Grace if we had an important person or churchman for lunch.

Mum's front garden, which we helped dig and the like, was a fenced-off section in front of the house where most things grew with fairly little attention. We had mint and rhubarb growing under the tap that brought water from the nearby windmill, and how we loved our rhubarb and apple pies. There were always some really nice coleus growing there. Sometimes we planted carrots and radishes, which were the easiest to grow, with the occasional bed of lettuce and tomatoes. Under the steps there was always a bed of violets, with white geraniums growing under the front veranda, and sometimes we planted packets of seeds – petunias, zinnias and snapdragons.

Music has always been a large part of my life. I started music lessons when we bought a piano (or *Goanna* as Dad called it) about the time I started at Milora School. I rode to Harrisville for lessons. About 2 pm on a Thursday I would saddle up my horse from the school paddock and head off the six miles for the Harrisville School of Arts. Dad gave me explicit directions the first time I rode to Harrisville from Milora when I was about 10 but I still got lost. I eventually arrived, going the long way around, and rode up Queen Street, Harrisville in tears. It was a very unhappy start to what would become a very happy musical career. After the lesson I rode home. While I was taught by Mrs Bode, or her son, Billy, my horse was tied up at the back of the School of Arts. I did my first theory exam when I was 11 and I remember the thrill of being able to make a treble clef on manuscript paper.

Other sisters rode the same road at different times. It was no easy job riding with a schoolbag on my back and a music case in one hand, bumping along as one cantered, possibly a switch in hand as well. Barb also had to carry her banjo-mandolin case. The neighbours, one lady in particular, kept Mum well and truly informed by phone about our progress en route from Harrisville to Radford, especially if we dawdled. I would be very averse to having a child riding solo on the roads these days, but back then it was rare to see a car or anyone on the 15-mile round trip. There were only a few houses on the route, as is still the case these days. If it was raining, we'd wear a cornsack for a raincoat, folded with a pixie-shaped hood for the head and tied with wire. (Sugar bags often came in handy – they could also be made into aprons and pot-holders.)

As I advanced on the piano, I sometimes caught the railmotor to Roadvale, Boonah or Teviotville for extra lessons before the practical exams held in Ipswich. Most of the kids in our family had the chance to learn music, some with more ability and enthusiasm than others. Dad was wont to break into song when working around the place at the least expected moments and I've inherited that trait. Some of the old songs I sing nowadays (in the 60 and Better Choir) are reminiscent of Dad's singing. As mentioned earlier, Dad was known to some of his old mates as Casey and I think of him every time we sing the song of that name. It is about a "Strawberry" blonde and, as Mum was a redhead, I wonder now if that inspired Dad to sing it so regularly.

When we bought our piano it was a mammoth job getting it up the front steps. Dad cursed the thing, but he had another shift getting it down the steps when it was given to me and I took it out West to Julia Creek. There was also a pianola at one time and Dad was again called upon to put his shoulder to the wheel. He was not overly fond of piano moving, but he was pretty strong. Dad didn't often complain, but when it came to piano moving he made an exception.

The only "entertainment" as we knew it on the farm was the wireless, an instrument about 30 inches high and nearly as wide, run off a wet battery (like a car battery). Dad absolutely *had* to listen to the news, so the rest of us had to use it carefully to leave it charged. We sat around the wireless, no-one daring to make a sound, in case Dad got angry, although we knew he was "all bark and very little bite". The war news was very important, but we were also allowed to hear the popular evening serials like *Martins' Corner, Dad and Dave* and *Search for the Golden Boomerang.* Dad took the wireless battery into Willmotts' Garage in Harrisville to be charged. Perhaps the lack of television had something to do with the big families in those days. People spent more time in conversation and Dad and Mum played euchre by kerosene light after the day's work was done.

During the war, when I was between four and 10 years old, the news was a most important item on the day's agenda. Dad, at 41 years old, wasn't eligible to join up when the war broke out as he was working in an important industry growing food, but on Sundays he went to Harrisville for Voluntary Defence Corps (VDC) training. Dad did join up in World War I, needing his parents' permission as he was under 21 years of age, but fortunately arrived overseas too late to see action. His ship, SS Bakara, was somewhere off Gibraltar when they received word that hostilities had ceased on November 11, 1918. He had the chance to see a bit of Europe and the British Isles though, which I imagine would have been a wonderful experience for a farm lad. In a letter to his father in March 1919 from Belgium, where he was stationed, he wrote: *I'll never see this side again, but I'll always be able to say I've seen the Old Country.* Dad enjoyed his holidays in Scotland. In his memoirs he said "all good things come to an end" when the leave was over. Dad returned from overseas on the SS Suevic, a more superior vessel, enjoying, as he said, "a very pleasant trip". It called in at several ports en route to Australia. The northern contingent disembarked at Melbourne and went by rail to Ipswich, where Dad was met by his mother. After he arrived home he was allowed one sleep-in, but the next morning Grandfather told him if he wanted to work on the farm he had better get up and get a move on.

We kids eagerly looked from our house on the hill for the dust of the car on his return from VDC training, because Dad always brought home a bundle of lemonade ice-blocks from McAway's shop. We didn't have a refrigerator at this stage so they were wrapped in several layers of newspaper to prevent their melting. He drove home with them as fast as possible, hence the good-sized cloud of dust. The worst part of VDC was the children's chore picking the burrs and prickles from his long khaki socks before they could be washed.

As kids we made our own fun on the farm. We played marbles, skipped if we could find a rope, spun tops and played house under our home, using any scraps that came to hand in an effort to appear domesticated. There was also a large tin trunk with treasures to be pored over. In fact, Mum gave me a cut-glass decanter from that trunk that I have probably never used, only looked at, but it must be well over 100 years old by now. Under the house there was also a "last" that Dad used to mend the soles of our shoes.

I remember playing with boxes made of pine in which we received our fruit from the Brisbane Markets or direct from the grower. I pretended that I was from Bayards' shop delivering goods to the farm. Mum held accounts with Cribb & Foote, Bayards and T.C. Beirne in Ipswich (all now no more). When in town she stocked up on household requirements and paid the accounts monthly. Shopping was parcelled up in brown paper and tied with string – no plastic bags. The string and paper were saved at home for use on another day.

We also liked playing in an old tank (which originally came from a ship) in which corn was kept under the house. We crawled inside the tank to scoop up the corn to feed the chooks and often stayed on down there to have a game. Imagine the dust, with only an opening about 15 inches in diameter at the top – it is a wonder we didn't all end up with lung complaints.

If by chance we had a ha'penny or a penny we'd wet the ground and rub the coin with our heels in the mud to get a lovely copper sheen on the coin. If anyone was digging post holes we took the clay out of the hole and modelled things, like people later used plasticine. It's amazing what amused a child in the days when toys were rare and you lived on the land. We had a sharpening stone, driven by pedals, with the pedaller sitting on a seat, and even though we didn't have "an axe to grind" we loved to sit and pedal. We usually sharpened sticks on it, and once or twice, someone else's finger.

Barbara went missing once, causing a great search on the farm and waterholes. Things were getting a little desperate when Mum heard a giggle from the big kitchen cupboard. There was Barb hiding from everyone. She also had a nap on a bag of sugar while the search was on. When Mirie was young she decided to run away and headed off for the front gate, with a few clothes in a little port and a couple of pennies. We persuaded her to come back before Mum and Dad got back from a car trip. They had been to see Ann in hospital.

Another risky bit of fun happened when Dad pulled up the casing out of the windmill bore that pumped water to the dairy, cattle troughs and our garden. Kath was particularly adept at walking across a narrow beam from the tank to the vanes of the mill, a distance of quite a few feet and at a good height. I was never game to do it, but Kath was unfazed. At least there was a wire above her head to hang on to. I often wonder how we all lived to tell the tale of games we played.

On a windy weekend we often made kites, or tried to, out of sticks and newspaper with flour and water paste. More often than not our kites barely lifted off the ground. I remember jumping off the front veranda holding an umbrella for a parachute. There were plenty of hard landings during our game. We also liked to make billycarts if we could find old wheels for the job. Very little was discarded in my younger days and everything was strongly built.

Our "daring deeds", besides galloping horses over huge logs, up and down steep creek banks and racing our horses on our way to school, included climbing trees. One was a huge bunya pine; we threw the nuts to mates below. There were some great mulberry trees on a farm we passed en route to school. On our return we climbed it and stuffed ourselves and our schoolbags. We often received punishment for ruining our clothing with mulberry juice, especially our white blouses.

On the way home from school one day we raided a loquat tree in the yard of a deserted farmhouse. About six of us were up the tree with our horses tied up to the fence when a huge, glowing ball of fire appeared to be heading straight for us from the west. We were down that tree quick as a flash – some parts of underwear still on the tree, having been torn asunder on the rough branches during our rapid descent – on the horses and headed for home flat strap. As we rode we heard a huge explosion. It turned out to be a meteorite. Barbara was at the "New Home" treadle sewing machine when she felt the machine shake and Mum heard the crockery in the kitchen rattle. When we told our tale to Mum she phoned the police, thinking it could have been someone up to no good, but the meteorite story became part of our folklore. Some even said it killed a cow or two and left a huge crater on landing somewhere in the Limestone Ridges area. (Research verifies it was a meteorite, seen from many places in southern Queensland about 4 pm on July 10, 1947, but I don't think it landed anywhere near us.) A couple of our friends on that wild ride home weren't believed and one mother took a strap to her children for telling lies to cover up being late home from school. We would have been even later if we hadn't received the shock of our lives and put our horses to the gallop.

We tried making bows and arrows at one stage, probably after John grew up a bit. Once when a few of us were confined to bed with a contagious disease (perhaps measles, mumps or chickenpox – we had 'em all) we devised a game using a phone book. The phone book was a new item around the house and we enjoyed looking up the names of all the people we knew in the district. I forget exactly how we played it, but it kept us out of Mum's hair for hours.

When the Warrill Creek flooded it filled the gully that flowed over the low-lying parts of our farm and did a lot of damage to crops and fences. Another hardship for the man on the land, but we kids saw it as an opportunity to swim, or should I say play, in the water near the gully at the bottom of our hill. The smattering of hard cow pats floating by didn't worry us. Naturally we had the sense not to go in the actual gully as it was quite swiftly flowing and we couldn't swim, but we played in the water in the clothes we were wearing. One day Mum came down the hill with a big switch and chased us all the way back to the house. We were probably told not to go in the water. It wasn't often we defied our parents.

We also swam in a creek on Carson's farm. The water was beautifully clear, but there was the odd leech. One day one of the girls (not me – but she who shall remain nameless) had a leech in a very private part. Big panic!! She was put on a chamber pot until the leech came out. I think she was taken to see Matron Pforr at the Harrisville Hospital. Matron was a legend, she could fix most things.

Toys were just about unheard of. Apparently I played with an empty box, and the stringy end of a Strasbourg sausage as a doll. I liked making dolls' houses with butter boxes, one on top of the other, with furniture made from matchboxes and cotton reels, but I don't think I was all that artistic. I was content to play on my own and still don't mind my own company. (I rarely, if ever, feel lonely.)

Used cardboard, crepe paper, cotton reels, tins and boxes were all made into "things", including presents. One Christmas, undeterred by the fact that we rarely used serviettes, I presented Mum with serviette rings made from cardboard and raffia! I can't remember Mum's reaction, but I guess she smiled and thanked me, as mothers do. I remember getting a ruler for

Christmas once, and one year Mum bought three undressed celluloid dolls for Kath, Mirie and me. I don't remember any other toys, except for a couple of spinning tops John and Rob received for Christmas once, but there were always some gifts at Christmas and possibly birthdays. One Easter, Mum's nephew brought us a box of little sugar Easter eggs, about two dozen eggs in all and a real treat. I cherished, and lamented the loss of, a glass money-box in the shape of a piano that someone gave me. It was my favourite gift, although second-hand. While it existed, my glass piano always had pride of place.

Often on a Sunday, the day of rest, we would pile into the Oldsmobile and go for a picnic, usually to a nice, clear stretch of Warrill Creek, where we could play in the water and eat to our heart's content while Dad snoozed under a tree.

Dad was rarely idle of course. Weekends were times for all sorts of jobs. One of them was to pump the tyres of our car by hand. We didn't have a tyre gauge so he counted the number of pumps going into each tyre to have even inflation. Dad was proud of the fact that he had never insured the Oldsmobile. He said he'd saved enough on insurance policies during the 22 years he had the Olds to buy a new car with the money. Luckily the old car never suffered damage or needed repairs.

When there was time between farmwork, Mum and Dad gave us some rudimentary dance lessons. This consisted of waltzing around the house, usually on the polished wooden floor of the sleep-out, with the old His Master's Voice wind-up gramophone supplying the music. This gave us an idea of the art before we were let loose among the grown-up dancers in the district. Dances were held in Harrisville, Peak Crossing, Warrill View, Munbilla and Kalbar. In fact most places had a hall used for dancing, Christmas trees and other functions, with pianos in practically all of them. Children often went to dances with their parents in those days, the smallest ones sleeping under the wooden forms that circled the hall, or up on the stage behind the piano. The bigger ones slid up and down the dance floor and at times attempted to dance while the adults were having a break between numbers.

The Grand Old Duke of York was a popular game, or dance, for the youngsters at church Christmas tree nights. A big branch cut from a tree in someone's paddock did for the tree and I can still recall the sight and smell. There was sometimes a supper room for a very welcome supper of delicious homemade cakes, sandwiches and a cup of tea halfway through the night. I don't remember having coffee in those days, but at home we had coffee essence in a bottle – never particularly popular.

If there was no supper room, men took tin tubs around the hall, full of sandwiches and cakes and the like, and some others with big pots of tea for the thirsty and hungry dancers. Alcohol was not allowed at dances in those days, but the men snuck out during the evening to have a snort, usually around the back of the hall in the dark.

Children did not normally go to the "balls", which were grander nights of dancing, but we attended concerts in the halls and the "pictures" at Harrisville. The local Harrisville girls gave us a hard time on occasion, usually kicking us through the canvas seats from behind.

If we had a planned outing, for instance a dance or the pictures, we kept an anxious eye on the sky all afternoon as storms or rain of any kind usually meant staying at home for fear of getting stuck on a wet road. It was a great disappointment if an outing was cancelled. The first strip of bitumen between our farm and Harrisville was a memorable event. We had the local Shire Chairman living near us at one time, which no doubt hastened the sealing of at least that part of the road from his place to Harrisville.

We had tennis courts at Radford and Milora schools so we had some experience playing and thought tennis might be a good idea for weekends. Dad ambitiously went for it. The grader driver who worked on the dirt roads in the district came to level out the designated area and the boys from the farm across the creek decided to come and lend a hand. Optimistically they brought their racquets with them! Dad drove our old Bedford truck to Mahaffey's paddock in search of ant-hills – the best surface for the purpose. He took the lads with him and they smashed up the large, hard ant heaps and loaded them on to the truck. What a job with only hand tools. After a couple of loads, Dad got a stake in a tyre and decided the tennis court wasn't such a good idea after all. We were very disappointed when the "good idea" did not come to fruition, and so were our optimistic helpers. In years to come the graded section proved a handy mounting block for equestrians and a loading ramp as well.

Lori aged 12 years under the peach tree.

Rob, Ann and John on the farm slide.

CHAPTER 4

Didn't We Have a Lovely Time

We had a lot of fun visiting our cousins, the Carsons, in Harrisville. They also had a dairy farm, although not as modern as ours. Aunty Mary was Mum's sister. You'd have to say that some of the Hollywood girls were good breeders because theirs was a large family too. Aunty Mary's family consisted of Alice, Hughie and Lonie (originally Loamside, being named after the railway siding where she was born), Winnie, Billy, Aileen, Juanita (June) and Ian (Pompey). I loved the Carsons' place for the big beds, each sleeping about four children. We went rollerskating on their big verandas, read comic books and, lying on our tummies on the verandas, fired air rifles into kerosene tins. One day Pompey got hit in the eye with a slug, but luckily there was no permanent damage.

The big table and couch near the kitchen fire intrigued me. It was nothing like our kitchen at home and gave a strange thrill at mealtimes. Singing around the piano was also a highlight. As we sang, a bevy of nude infants looked down at us from their large picture frames. Barrie later said his most lasting memory of the Carsons' house was Pomp singing "Bless This House".

Hughie Carson was a great piano-accordion player and in demand as a musician at district dances. In all his years as a local entertainer, I can't remember him ever using a music book, and the musical gift is obvious in some of the younger Carsons today.

At the Carsons' house in the big metropolis of Harrisville it was a treat to walk over to the shops to buy a sarsaparilla ice-block! The rail line bisected Carsons' farm, and we enjoyed watching the trains and railmotor pass by. We sometimes took a kitten home after a visit to the Carsons but Dad was afraid of a child being smothered and if he found a cat on a bed or pillow he'd take it out and shoot it. We had a few cats over the years. On Saturdays or school holidays the Carson kids sometimes came to our place on the 10.30am railmotor and went home on the 2.30pm service.

I loved going to Grandma and Grandfather Harsant's place too. They lived near the school and the Radford railway station and made a fuss of me when I was small. Grandma Harsant was a very placid, kind lady whom we all loved. Grandmother had a proper big white enamel bath, whereas we only had a large, round tin tub, usually on the side veranda, but brought inside and placed near the kitchen stove in winter. I loved it when Grandma's housemaid washed and dried me and my feet felt like a baby's. Made me wonder why I didn't get the same treatment at home, but I should have realised that our maid would have had much more to do in our busy household.

In later years when staying over we took candles to bed, which had to be blown out early "for economy's sake" and for us to be sufficiently rested and ready for Grandfather's early wake-up call. At 4.30am he could be relied on to stomp around the house yelling at everyone to get up with the wireless going full blast ready for the first news of the day – ABC Radio of course. (I must take after Grandfather Harsant because the first thing I do on waking is switch on the radio, tuned to the ABC naturally.) Before leaving our warm beds we sang our own lyrics to the news intro tune: *The wind blew up his trouser leg and around his "fiddely dee"*.

Grandfather then chopped chips and wood on the back landing to light the stove. Eventually the landing had to be replaced, so hacked about with a tomahawk or axe was it. Uncle Cedric, who lived there too, rose early also. He milked the house cow, bringing the warm milk up to the house for breakfast.

At the meal table in the old homestead, Grandma kept the flies away from the food by sprinkling pepper on the tablecloth, especially in the middle of the day. I don't know whether it was effective, but she had faith in the practice. I wondered why I'd sometimes see Grandma Harsant asleep on a cane daybed after lunch, but realise now that she would also have been woken at "sparrow's", the same as the rest of the household.

One school holiday during the war, Dad drove Mirie and me to stay with Aunty Jean and Uncle George at Highgate Hill in Brisbane. That was really special. They later shifted to the neighbouring suburb of West End. Uncle George was a very stern character, and we dared not put a foot out of place. He used the same lunch wrapper of brown paper and string for at least a week. Every night when he arrived home by tram he put the wrapping neatly folded on to the china cabinet ready for the morning. People were very conscious of "waste not, want not" in the 1940s. Before moving to Brisbane, Uncle George had a carpentry business in Gordonvale and now he worked in the mail-sorting section of the GPO.

Mirie and I sat on a brick fence down the road and watched the trams go by. I remember being roused at by the people in the house who owned the fence for making too much noise. Sometimes we went by tram to the city with Aunty Jean and Grandma Hollywood to look at the shops. While they were shopping, Mirie and I would spend the time riding up and down the escalators. That was a good game and we loved going to the Shingle Inn for lunch. Once Grandma Hollywood caught her heel in the tramlines in Queen Street and we had to help get her unstuck. With a tram heading for us there was a big panic. That wasn't our only close encounter with a tram. Dad sometimes had occasion to take us to Brisbane in the old car. He took a wrong turn one day and a tram driver stuck his head out of the door and said, "Get off the bloody tramline". Dad replied, "Get off the bloody thing yourself".

A couple of times I stayed with Aunt Andrina and Uncle Eric Payne at Ashgrove for the August holidays. We rode the trams from Ashgrove to the city, an eagerly awaited bit of excitement. As well as a day at the Ekka, we spent a week at their shack at Golden Beach, Caloundra. Their boys, Everett, Graeme and Neil, and I slept in a tent. Later they put a cottage on the block. These times with my three cousins were happy times. Getting there was fun, with an old tourer car packed to the gunwales with blankets and food and a lot of the luggage in ex-army metal ammunition boxes on the running boards. It took about three hours to get from Ashgrove to Caloundra, a trip of about one hour today. The fishing was good and we had fun cooking on a small fire on the beach. Neil was usually the cook, and the fish were often as small as six inches long. (Sadly Neil lost his life in later years while diving off the Northern NSW coast.)

Mirie and I travelled to New South Wales by rail in the Christmas holidays of 1950, disembarking at Hornsby where we were met by Mum's brother, Uncle Bob Hollywood, and his wife, Aunt Bessie. We enlarged our education with an enjoyable six week holiday in Kenthurst and the surrounding district, including a couple of trips to the city of Sydney and Taronga Zoo. Our cousin, Tim, drove us in his father's car to catch the ferry to the zoo. The road rules must have been stricter than those of Queensland because a couple of us had to hide on the floor of the car under a blanket while in the Sydney traffic, a most enlightening experience for a pair of kids from a dairy farm. It was here that I first came across the rivalry between States. Our cousin said, "You can smell Queensland as soon as you cross the border from New South Wales, even if you're flying". That attitude might still be held in certain quarters, especially when it comes to Rugby League.

The Hollywoods, who also had a daughter, Nola, owned and lived on a poultry and fruit farm. I struck up a friendship with one of Tim's mates, who wrote to me after we came back to Radford. Dad read the letter and it gave him a great deal of amusement. It started out *Dear Sweatheart.* "He can't even spell!" Dad protested.

When I was about 12, I was all packed ready to go to a Presbyterian Fellowship Association Camp at Alexandra Headland on the Sunshine Coast. It was cancelled at the last minute because some idiot let the water out of the rainwater tanks. I was greatly disappointed.

We regularly welcomed visitors to the farm. Our lovely cousin, Judy Donaldson from Melbourne, stayed with us on a holiday of recuperation from an illness. She was the daughter of Mum's sister, Vera, and she brightened our lives and widened our horizons. I thought our cousin Judy was the most wonderful person I'd ever met and was impressed when she took to horseriding like a duck to water. She gave me a book called *Children of the New Forest,* which to this day is my favourite book of all time. When I was 17, Judy also lent me a strapless, glittering, blue ball gown that I wore with elbow-length gloves. When I was ready to step out to a ball, Dad told me I looked as if I had the dress on the wrong places. It was fairly revealing for his taste. However, I passed muster and went off for a good night of dancing. Whenever Mum and Dad set off for a dance or ball they had a small glass of sherry. That night they offered me a nip. It was four years before the legal drinking age and a signal that they realised I was growing up. Judy spent quite a few holidays with us.

Once we had a visitor from New Zealand, Olive Rutherford. Aunt Olive we called her. Noting my interest in music, she gave me the sheet music for a Maori song called "Waiata Poi" and taught me to play it on the piano and sing it. I can still remember most of the song, although the sheet music was lost many moons ago. It was my first piece of sheet music, written by Alfred Hill in 1904.

We Harsant kids were millionaires, not much money, but plenty of the important things in life. Good parents, good food and the freedom of a country upbringing. I have heard some of my near and dear ones say, when I consider spending a bit of money, "You're not a Depression kid any longer! If you want it, buy it". We were brought up with an inbuilt conservatism when it comes to spending money. You get like that when there is none to spare. You never threw anything away that might possibly be of use later. We found that also applied in the West during the 20 or so years we lived out past Longreach. You never knew when something might "come in handy", or when or from where you could get another one, owing to the tyranny of distance from the shops. The old motto applied – repair not replace.

Lori with a friend in Sydney, 1950.

CHAPTER 5

Holy Snight

In my childhood we went to the "seaside" – now people go to the "coast".

Scarborough or Queens Beach at Redcliffe north of Brisbane were our family's popular holiday destinations and we went for a couple of weeks each year. We'd have the ute loaded up with kids, our few clothes, a large container of homemade biscuits, cooked chooks and vegies from the farm such as pumpkins, potatoes, beetroot and beans, and Dad usually stopped at a farm near Redcliffe to get a case of grapes. (We normally bought fruit by the case.) A highlight of the car trip was the Hornibrook Bridge, and we waited with excitement for that part of the trip to experience the bump in the middle. The suspension in the old car caused a good jolt. Sometime in later years when there wasn't enough room for us all in the ute two or three kids went by train to Sandgate where Dad picked them up. We had a train line from Boonah to Ipswich then, so could get on the railmotor at Radford.

We thought the waves at Scarborough Beach were tremendous. (What a shock to see ocean beaches later in life. Caloundra was the first surfing beach I saw.) There were usually a few cases of sunburn and Mum cut a potato in half and rubbed it on the affected skin for relief. The beds were pretty old and saggy, usually with two or three of us to a bed.

One year at Scarborough Mum sent three of us to a Redcliffe shop to get cough mixture for a sick kid. Of course we dallied on the big pier and one of us dropped the purse containing a 10-shilling note into the briny. We turned back to the holiday house in tears. Along the way we met our school teacher, "Jolly" Jenkins. When we told him of our dilemma he gave us the money for the required medicine. We were so anxious to get home with it that we dropped the bottle and it smashed. Cough mixture all over the cement footpath. There was hell to pay – I can't remember the repercussions, but Mum was very, very cranky.

There was no bridge to Bribie Island in those days and we went on a day trip from Redcliffe to Bribie Island on the SS Koopa.

I began my "singing career" in Redcliffe. We were hanging around the skating rink. Watching the rollerskating at Redcliffe was a favourite pastime. We never had a go, but watched enviously. Someone was giving out free ice-creams to anyone who could sing a Christmas carol. We lined up and I sang "Silent Night". I received a three-penny cone of ice-cream and was very proud of myself. Dad teased me and said I sang *Holy Snight* instead of *Holy Night*. Perhaps the experience was encouraging, because in later years I often sang, or played the piano, in Billy Bode's concerts in the halls about the district.

One year before we headed off to Scarborough, our neighbour, Mrs Rayner, who was a very clever seamstress, made us girls shorts in seaside print cotton with anchors, shells, ropes, etc. Two pairs each did us for the whole holiday. Mrs Rayner also made our good dresses. A photo of us taken in a Redcliffe studio shows some of her handiwork. On another occasion we were given new sandals. There was a cobbler, or bootmaker, in Harrisville by the name of Ted Faulkner who, as well as repairing shoes, made leather sandals. Mum had him make a pair for some of us at 10 shillings a pair. (As I write this Ted

Faulkner still lives in the same building in Harrisville's main street and must be a good old age.)

Another memorable holiday was a week at Spicer's Gap on the Great Dividing Range, not too far from the home farm. We set off for a hut up there on Boxing Day 1944, loaded up with enough food for a week. We even took a few live chooks and ducks to keep up the meat supply. There were no shops, electricity or refrigeration, in fact not even a road, merely a rough bush track. Dad drove the Oldsmobile ute, with the poultry in a wire cage, and Mum drove Grandfather's Studebaker Tourer. Sometimes we kids would get out and put rocks behind the back wheels of the Studebaker if it was having difficulty negotiating some of the rough terrain, which included steep gullies. Mum handled the rough going with aplomb.

Spicer's Gap was a glorious place, full of adventure, walking through the bush, seeing huge pythons and goannas, listening to bell birds and whip birds, and walking to the "Governor's Chair", a large, rocky outcrop. Not far from there we could see the traffic, in miniature, headed for Cunningham's Gap to cross over to the Darling Downs. The "gap" is through two mountains – Mitchell and Cordeaux. Dad told us of a time when he and Mum lived near the main road, now called the Cunningham Highway, on the Ipswich side of the gap. They went away for a couple of weeks' holiday, I don't know to where, and when they arrived home they discovered that although they'd accidentally left the house unlocked, not a thing had been touched. That was during the big Depression, when many men walked the roads looking for work, or a feed. There must have been a lot of honest swaggies then.

After doing my scholarship exam (the equivalent of Year 8, but a big deal then), I went to Ipswich Girls' Grammar School (IGGS) as a boarder. I really liked it. Out of the four of us who went to boarding school, I think I was the only one who enjoyed it. Of course going up the elegant school driveway in the ancient Oldsmobile was a bit of an embarrassment. (It was offset by learning that some of the other girls' parents didn't even own a car.) Later that year, it was with a huge sigh of relief that I saw Dad drive up to collect me in the new second-hand black sedan. His 1934 Pontiac was as good as a limo to me.

Music and English were my favourite subjects, but on the whole, I was only a very average student. Music was my inspiration. I imagined I could end up like Eileen Joyce, a celebrated pianist at the time, and never needed any encouragement to practise. Enthusiasm was high (and ignorance was bliss). I joined the photography group, and took some shots with Mum's old Box Brownie. (Recently I took photos of the same mountains with my new digital camera and the contrast amazes me. I have done a digital photography course and continue the hobby I started in 1949.)

As far as I was concerned, the food and living conditions at IGGS were fine. Some girls might have led a more salubrious life, but it was no hardship to me. The highlight of boarding school for me was the lovely girls I roomed with and sometimes took home to the farm for weekends. In my first year these were Nita Hirning and Noela Lee, and in my second year twins Barbara and Jackie Shinnie and Barbara McVey. One holiday I went to Maleny for a week with a friend, Helen Rowe. Her father was the manager of the butter factory.

On Saturdays we lined up in Miss Carter's study to get our little purses from an old suitcase and take out sixpence, the amount allowed for tuckshop. Miss Carter wrote down the amount in a book, to keep tabs on our spending at the corner shop across at the nearby Five Ways. Sometimes, if we thought there was enough in kitty, we would ask for more money to buy toothpaste, shoe polish or some other extra, whether needed or not, to buy more than our sixpence worth of lollies. This was my first experience of pocket-money.

On Sundays we were given a piece of cake and a piece of fruit for afternoon tea. I committed my first (and I think only) stealing offence one Sunday afternoon when a lot of us were dared to "steal" a piece of fruit each before the afternoon tea bell went. Of course we were found out and had to front up to

Miss Carter. She lectured us in her office and said she was going to punish us severely. In the end she said, "You may go now, girls". No punishment was delivered, but I was terrified that Mum and Dad would be notified.

We had the day girls take home a tin of condensed milk for their mothers to cook in a pressure cooker, providing a yummy caramel sweet eaten surreptitiously with a finger in the music block locker room where we kept our music books.

One day at Grammar when some of us were sitting on a stone wall, a baker's horse went mad and raced through the grounds, dragging the breadcart behind, loaves flying everywhere. It was followed by the owner and the police. Boarding school was full of fun for me.

I was a low-grade tennis player, in the C Grade team, and thoroughly enjoyed the interschool competition, especially when we caught the train from East Ipswich Station to Brisbane to play against the big boarding schools. The Annual Interschool Sports in Brisbane at the Exhibition Grounds was a day of great fun, and I was in the relay and the ball-games teams. In all, a very average sportswoman, but the trips to Brisbane made a welcome change.

I can't remember the names of all my teachers at IGGS, but Miss Carter (also known as Kitty) was the headmistress, bless her little socks. We called the raspberry jam we were served "Patsy's fleas in blood", after the previous head's little dog, Patsy. There was also Misses Benson, Brown, Brady, Kennedy, Marsden, Pratt and Mrs Green the music teacher, another dear soul, and Matron Kilner. There were no male teachers on the staff. Alas, for all their efforts, as I said earlier, I was a very average student.

My older sisters, Margaret and Kathleen, didn't go to boarding school, but went to Cairns in Far North Queensland to stay with our Aunt Kathleen and Uncle Les. They attended Cairns State High and did their Junior exams there, but my younger sisters, Mirie and Ann, went to IGGS as I did. None of my siblings went on to senior or university but Barbara, who had boarded at Brisbane Girls' Grammar, went into nursing. (This required a lot of study and as a mature-age student she also did a university course.) The rest of the girls in our family became clerks and governesses. My brothers, John and Rob, remained men of the land, farming and grazing.

While I attended IGGS, Barbara was nursing at the Ipswich General Hospital. She came to see me at weekends and, as a bonus, brought me sweets. It was a bit of a coup to have a visitor. She was probably better off resting on her time off instead of visiting me, but we enjoyed each other's company.

Going to church on Sundays was a good way to get out of the school grounds for a couple of hours. A teenager called Hubert Cornish, whose father was the minister at St Paul's, was keen on one of the other Church of England boarders, and often followed us up the hill back to school on his pushbike. When television arrived in Queensland on August 16, 1959, Hugh became a television celebrity as the first newsreader in the state.

It was good having a couple of hours off to go to Confirmation Classes after school on a weekday, leading up to my confirmation at St Paul's. During one of the classes the tallest girl in our group was baptised there, which was quite interesting. She had to be baptised, of course, before she could be confirmed.

One thing that comes to mind about Grammar is the black lisle stockings that were part and parcel of the uniform. When they laddered they had to be mended and that was a fiddly job. Of course in those days we always mended ladders in our nylons too, sometimes using a hair out of one's head for thread. Clothes were always mended to serve another day, including our knickers.

While I was at Grammar I found that practically all of the girls had an autograph book, the most important signatures and verses being those of fellow pupils. Of course I had to have one, and later my dorm mates also kindly gave me a photograph album for my birthday in my Junior year, which I still have, although it's somewhat dilapidated now.

One birthday I was called to Miss Carter's office to receive a parcel, and of course it had to be opened in her presence. It was a gift sent by Kath from Cairns, where she was working for our uncle, Les Archibald, in his Express Parcel business, and the packet contained a tube of lipstick. Make-up was usually frowned upon before a girl reached 16 years of age and was certainly not allowed at Grammar School. "Kitty" kicked up a fuss. She was adamant that my lipstick was not to be used on school premises. I agreed, and managed to persuade Miss Carter to let me keep it by saying that on holidays I spent a great deal of time riding horses and it would be beneficial as a sunblock. It was the first cosmetic product I'd ever owned.

Family portrait taken on holidays at Redcliffe.

CHAPTER 6

The Milk Maid

Just before my 16th birthday, after completing a Junior Level commercial course at Grammar, I returned to work on the farm. Dad was in poor health and needed help with the tractor work, dipping and milking. I wasn't the only daughter to help out between school and other employment. Barbara and Mirie also did a stint. "Working men" were non-existent by this time. In our large family the sooner you went to work the better. Further education wasn't seen as an option. Dad, after all, had left school at 14.

By now of course some of the girls were scattered far and wide and the boys still too young to work on the farm. The operation of the farm had changed with the years, but the dairy was still the main source of income and it meant an early start. Dad rose at 4.30am and when he called, "Get out of bed!" there were no excuses and no exceptions. He'd make a pot of tea on the primus stove and put out the bread and butter for a snack before we started work. It tasted great. We never had sliced bread in those days, and one could cut off a great doorstop slab and slather it in chunks of butter. There's no doubt sliced bread was a great invention, but it didn't compare to the old double loaf with the join in the middle "where the bread kisses". After this satisfying start to the day I saddled up the night horse and headed off to round up the milkers. As soon as we left the house we called the cows, so by the time I'd ridden behind them they were on their feet and walking towards the dairy.

The cows rested in the gullies or down on the flat where Dad relocated an old cottage from Munbilla. That cottage has since been renovated by my brother, Rob, and his wife, Jan, and is used as a weekender for paying guests. Alec Brook, one of the workers who'd once lived in the cottage, said our house on the hill was a flannel shirt warmer than his cottage. The flannel shirts worn in "the old days" were different from the modern cotton flannelette. The old flannel shirt was made of rough woollen material, often with no collar and with short sleeves. Grandfather Harsant wore a cream-coloured one, but they were mostly grey.

Milking was a very uncomfortable chore in the winter, with frost thick on the ground and often a dense fog. I can't remember having gloves early on, but owing to our quiet nags, hands in the pockets was the way to go. We wore high rubber boots with thick socks. After the milking and during the cleaning up, I half-filled a five-gallon drum with hot water and stood in it to get my feet warm. At times I even stood in newly produced hot cow manure to get some warmth – in the boots, of course. After the milking was done, we grazed the cows on a lucerne paddock for an hour. That was called "minding the cows". We then returned to the house for breakfast, after which I would either get on the tractor to plough a paddock, mow an area of lucerne to be raked and taken to the shed for making into chaff afterwards, or do one of the many other jobs around the farm, including shifting heavy irrigation pipes.

If working near the house, we had lunch there. The long-running radio serial *Blue Hills* aired every day at 1pm and we never missed an episode if we were in the house. It was about country people, so it particularly resonated with us farmers. If I was ploughing for the day I took my lunch with me – sandwiches wrapped in newspaper and black tea with a generous helping of sugar in an old softdrink bottle. Dad had his work cut out teaching me to plough. I had trouble on the corners of the paddocks and Dad would get frustrated and yell at me. When I finally got the hang of it he was pleased. After a dusty day's ploughing, a bath was most welcome. I had the idea once that it would be nice to dress for dinner. Mum dismissed this idea as an extravagance that only added to the laundry work. "Dad can change out of his short-sleeved flannel shirt into a cotton one," I protested, but no, I had to get straight into my pyjamas after a bath.

I had a fairly busy social life – mainly pictures, dances and playing the piano or the piano-accordion at concerts or Presbyterian Fellowship Association functions. We were Anglicans, but the McFarlanes, local farmers who gave us a lift to town, were Presbyterians so we joined in all their activities. At this stage I was too young to get my driver's licence. My farm wages paid for clothes and outings. A girl usually had only one or two good frocks in the '40s and '50s. A dress could cost more than a week's wages, so one had to save for the purchase, and stockings, gloves and hats were necessities for the well-dressed girl. No credit cards or time-payment when I was young, but you could use "lay-by", a last resort, but welcome at times. I was very touched when Dad bought me a leather skirt and waistcoat from a travelling salesman, quite uncharacteristic for Dad who, despite the predominance of the fairer sex in our household, avoided anything to do with female apparel.

Around this time I was "going out" with a Peak Crossing lad called Doug Forsyth. One night Doug took me to the pictures in his parents' old tourer car, circa 1928. After travelling for a few miles we heard a noise in the back and up popped his sister, Dulcie. She'd hidden under a blanket in the back of the car. It gave us a heck of a fright. It couldn't have been too comfortable for her in the old vehicle, but she'd lasted under that blanket for 10 miles before discovery.

Sometimes I went to a ball or other social occasion that ended in the early hours of the morning. The next day I was inclined to nod off on horseback. This was OK on the quiet horses, but we had one frisky pony called Nixie who caused me grief. Dad sent him to the Rayner's property for several weeks to be broken in. After breaking-in proved impossible, Dad brought the thin little thing home and gave me the job. After leaving the saddle for the dirt several times and looking up into the eyes of the wilful horse, Nixie eventually became reasonably well behaved and, except for the odd indiscretion, proved somewhat useful.

Further down the track, brother John rode Nixie to a cattle sale in Harrisville, his Brisbane friend, Ewan Macgregor-Lowndes, accompanying him on another horse. Mum received a call from John saying, "Can you come and pick us up, I've sold the horses". He was rather pleased because he received £10 ($20) for each horse. But a couple of days later Dad received a phone call from the buyer, complaining that the pony was impossible to ride. He claimed he'd bought the pony under the impression it was quiet because the auctioneer had said that the city boy from Brisbane could ride him. He demanded his money back. "I gave no guarantees," Dad responded, "the horse is yours." The new owner must have given up the fight because eventually I heard that Nixie joined a travelling rough-riding show.

I was still taking piano lessons once a week and did a fair bit of practice. During this time I rode the old pushbike for lessons at the Warrill View Hall, often having a close encounter with the "dog" trailer of a fast-moving semi. I reached Grade 6 and playing Chopin's "Military Polonaise", "Black and White Rag", "Calico Rag" and music of that ilk. However, I gave up lessons when I started work in Ipswich.

When I was 16, I bought a piano-accordion. It belonged to a cousin, Lonie Carson, a young mother who sadly died of poliomyelitis. Dad paid £40 for it, and out of my weekly pay of £2 ($4) I repaid 10/- ($1). I don't think I ever made all the repayments. It was money well spent – it lasted me many years. (I eventually replaced it with the accordion that I still play today. Two piano-accordions in over 60 years is pretty good going.) I taught myself to play the base buttons in front of the mirror.

After my sister, Kath, returned from Cairns, she obtained a job in the office of the *Queensland Times* (*QT*) newspaper in Ipswich. Little did I know that Kath's new job would change my life for ever.

On a picnic with the boyfriends.

CHAPTER 7

Romance Blooms

After Mirie left boarding school she came home to take over my job on the farm and I joined Kath to work at the *Queensland Times*. When I went to the job interview for the position of clerk-typist with front-counter duties, I first heard Dad's old saying "Take a cut lunch, you might get a start". I had taken dressmaking lessons at the Ipswich Technical College and to make a good impression I made myself a new dress to wear, a pale-salmon cotton number. Unfortunately, I ran over a fresh pile of hot cow manure during the ride on my battered old bike to the Radford Station to catch the railmotor. The bike had no mudguards and my beautiful new dress collected a fresh, steamy lucerne by-product. With the aid of a hanky, Kath and I cleaned the dress under the tap of the station's rainwater tank and I went off in a wet dress on the 6.50am railmotor.

On arrival at the *Queensland Times* office I met all the office staff, including James Barrie Patrick, the son of Ern, the sub-editor of the paper. Barrie was one of the clerk-typists, and being a bit of a joker said, "I can smell the cow yard".

I was embarrassed and thought we'd failed to clean my dress, but he later said that he couldn't really smell anything and was making a joke about country girls like us coming to the city because he'd never met real "country bumpkins" before. I was appointed on the spot and Kath and I arrived back home after work around 7pm, a long day.

The *QT* was strategically situated on the corner of Ellenborough and Brisbane streets. I spent a lot of my time on the front counter as well as working the switchboard. The front counter was particularly busy because our customers paid by cash or cheque. Besides account payments, we took a lot of classified ads; these were also dictated to us over the phone. One day we had a good laugh after a food manufacturer phoned in with an ad: *Wanted to buy, Mangoldwurzels*. It's a type of beet usually used as cattle food, but also used as "faux" fruits to go in jams and mixed-fruit products.

Wages came in little envelopes, so making up the pays was a pretty big job. I often had to accompany someone to the bank to pick up the money for the weekly pays, and I walked to the bank daily with the day's takings. Banking hours were 10am to 3pm weekdays. Work was a lot more hands-on and messages and accounts were run around town on foot by a junior member of staff such as me. Photos were sent to Brisbane by train in the morning, converted into plates and returned later in the day for inclusion in the following day's paper, which was printed on site. We always took our lunch to work; our modest wages meant that "bought" lunches were real treats. The North Star Hotel across the road was a popular haven for the menfolk of the *QT*. I don't recall the girls ever going to the pub, but perhaps there were some exceptions I didn't hear about.

Kath and I were quite a novelty for a while, having to tell everybody at work about life on a farm. Barrie thought he had a bit of knowledge of horses because his mate, Noel "Nugget" Mills, owned one and the milkman once did too. That was when the town milkman put the milk into a billy-can on the back porch. Barrie's "Nana", Annie Hughes, also drove a horse in a sulky before he was born. That was all Barrie knew about horses! Cars were also a rarity those days in Pommer Street, Brassall, where the Patricks lived. Nearly everybody caught the bus.

Just before I met Barrie he'd had his appendix removed and he enjoyed showing off his scar, saying he couldn't lift the heavy typewriters for the females in the office in case it exacerbated the wound. Actually my sister, Barbara, met Barrie before I did, having nursed him in the Ipswich General Hospital at the time of the big operation. "Mind the operation!" he would say, "Mind the operation!" His huge scar was impressive. It was an inherited complaint. His mother and her mother both had pelvic appendix, with big scars caused by peritonitis after almost leaving it too late to have the operations.

While working on the farm I polished up my driving in the 1934 Pontiac sedan but didn't get my licence until my 17th birthday on April 1, 1952. I took a day off work from the QT to go to the Harrisville Police Station to do the test. The local constable had previously turned his back if I happened to drive to the shops in Harrisville to get supplies or do other errands, but now it was time to become a legal driver.

I did a few manoeuvres then "the Sarge" said I'd passed and gave me the precious piece of paper. There were no electric blinkers on the earlier-model cars and all signals were made by the arm and hand out the window, either straight out for a right hand turn or over the top of the car for a left-hand turn and the obvious for a stop. No seatbelts either. Dad roused at me for telling the sergeant that the handbrake was faulty when I had a bit of trouble on a steep-hill start. I felt as if I needed three feet for the three pedals. "I could get fined for that," Dad said. Ironically the officer testing me didn't himself have a licence; his mode of transport around his bailiwick was in the sidecar of a motorcycle ridden by his constable.

I was one of the few with a licence in the office. One day I was given the job of driving a QT ute to pick up something that couldn't be carried on foot. I wasn't overly confident, but didn't admit it and got through the chore safely.

Our parents were very good in lending us girls the car. We went from the 1927 Oldsmobile to a Pontiac circa 1935 and ended up with a new Austin A40 sedan. Kath, Mirie and I were coming home from a ball in Harrisville at about 2am one night with Kath driving when we got a puncture near Parcell's Farm. We stripped down to our petticoats, put the ball gowns in the car and changed the tyre in the moonlight. Saturdays were the highlight of the week. We arrived home from Saturday morning work obligations just before 1pm and spent the afternoon washing our hair and ironing our clothes. Our big starched petticoats, which were all the fashion, were the most time-consuming.

I continued to play the piano and before long Mirie, Kath and I formed a trio. Mirie bought a second-hand drum kit that she played; Kath played the piano-accordion and I played piano at dances and concerts. Our little group was of limited ability but had plenty of enthusiasm. One year our trio entered the Ipswich Railway Rostrum Talent Quest and came second. Colleen Pennell, a gifted violinist, won the contest. The heats were lunch-hour concerts on the Rostrum at the Railway Workshops and the finals were held at the Ipswich Town Hall with a capacity audience.

Barrie and I started to go out together and I was often invited to spend the weekend at the Patricks' home. Once when we were going to the pictures in Ipswich early in our courting days, the chap next-door offered us a lift in his little sports car. But on the way he ran up the back of a poorly lit horse and sulky. Its only illumination was an old kerosene lantern hanging from the axle under the vehicle. There was still the occasional horse-drawn vehicle getting around at that time. We were forced to catch a bus, and as we were boarding we saw the poor old horse with harness attached (but no sulky) standing at the door of a blacksmith's in Down Street. The horse was shaking and holding up one hind leg as if in pain or fright. It was sheer luck that it happened near the blacksmith shop.

When I first met Barrie he went to about three dances a week and was very proficient on the dance floor. He went with his mate, Noel Mills. They'd eye off all the girls, especially the "good sorts". Nobody must have caught his eye, as he picked me eventually. He mostly gave up dances for the pictures when we started going out together. Dancing three nights a week, playing rugby league and going to work five and a half days a week was enough to keep a young man fairly fit and out of mischief.

As we girls matured, our dairy was a popular place for the "boyfriends". After one of Mum's big Sunday lunches (at washing-up time), our menfolk adjourned to the dairy to have a beer or two. The beaux, who weren't aware of the history or workings of the dairy, liked to sit around on the milking blocks (comprised of tree trunks sawn at a height suited to the milker and the cow) drinking their beers and telling tall stories. Once when Dad went to start the milking, beer bottles were hanging off the teat cups of the machines in all the cow bails. (In our day, we called the teats "tits" – the more refined term came into fashion after the Department of Agriculture and Stock became more sophisticated.) It was lucky for our fellows that Dad had a placid nature – most times. He was very fond of our fellows and that feeling was reciprocated. "Old Radford" they called Dad.

While Barrie and I were courting we went to creeks and waterholes for picnics or a swim at the weekends with Kath and her beau (and future husband), George Keidge, a motor mechanic of good repute. We usually had the younger kids of my family in tow, keeping an eye on us – playing gooseberry. The piano-accordions were often taken along for entertainment.

Most of our "fun" was had virtually for the price of a bit of petrol. Before buying his 1932 Ford V8 sedan, George had a Matchless motorbike and came up to the farm with Barrie as pillion passenger. Barrie said it was so cold on the motorbike that if he spat it'd freeze and nearly knock out a fence post, so Kath and I knitted balaclava caps for the boys. I don't remember there being bike helmets in those days, unless they were made of leather. We were pretty good knitters, having had plenty of practice during the war and while sitting on the railmotor to and from work.

George and Kath and Barrie and I often went to dances together. One occasion was a fancy dress evening. Barrie came in a pram, one leg on either side, dressed as a baby, bonnet and all, with mustard pickles spread over the nappy draped over the pram. He was sucking a teat on a large beer bottle. I don't know what was in the bottle! George, dressed as a large-breasted lady, was pushing the pram and they called themselves "Ma and Little Gertrude". But it was Kath and I who won a prize that night. We dressed in old-fashioned bathing costumes and called ourselves *Mr and Mrs Southport 1899*.

The four of us had a lot of fun together. On another night we went to a dance in Harrisville and Barrie and I decided to go and sit in the car until Kath and George were ready to leave the dance. We sat there for ages (talking of course) wondering why they hadn't turned up. When they did they told us they'd had trouble finding us and that actually we were sitting in the wrong car! It was a replica of the Harsant A40 and an easy mistake to make, because no-one locked their car in those days and most of the A40s were a green colour.

George also played rugby league in the same Railways team as Barrie when they were younger. Folklore has it that their line was uncrossed in 1950 when their team was undefeated premiers. Barrie eventually "retired" from football, but before he did, I attended Saturday matches at the North Ipswich Reserve with his mother, Eva, and sat with the mothers of the other players.

We sisters and our beaux often socialised together. At one party, one of the boys saw a big green grub in a salad dish. He put it between two pieces of cheese, and offered it to a friend who was very partial to a nice piece of cheese. A comedy act was being performed at the time and the cheese-eater took a bite, but was so interested in the comedienne he didn't see the big grub wriggling out of the cheese. Next big mouthful and cheese and grub were gone. Before our very eyes!! I thought it was disgusting, but the boys thought it was hilarious. I think it was the night the boys decided to "christen" the tyres of a guest's car parked outside the house where the party was being held. The car was a limo that delivered a high-up politician. I think he was a party leader, or Premier or some such. The young people in those days were a pretty law-abiding lot and never went beyond the occasional practical joke.

All the brothers-in-law to-be enjoyed a bit of harmless fun, like going to the pub "for a few". We sometimes had a couple of dozen people for lunch at the farm on weekends, including city friends and the boyfriends. One day after lunch they decided to go to the Harrisville pub, but one of the sisters put a stop to that and hid all the car keys. Dad was very annoyed and told us to behave and hand over the keys. We never dreamt of disobeying our dad. Another time they went to the Rosevale Pub for a drink, and one beau (not Barrie) thought he was a cowboy and jumped on the back of a cow that was standing near the pub veranda. The boyfriend was a townie, so I don't know how long he survived his big bullride. Ride'em, Cowboy Keith!

A special treat while we were courting was tasting our first Have-a-Heart ice-creams. These first made an appearance at the Brisbane Exhibition.

Around this time Barrie and I bought a block of land in Hayes Street, Brassall, from Mrs Hunter, who would become my sister Barbara's mother-in-law. On weekends we walked from Patrick's place to the allotment armed with all the tools needed to clear it – picks, shovels, crowbar, etc. We didn't have a motor vehicle (or "wheels" as Barrie and Nugget Mills enviously referred to them) so our transport was by "shanks' pony" and loads could be heavy. We bought the allotment for £40 ($80). We thought we made a fortune when we sold it in 1957 for £140. A short time later, allotments in that area went for £1400 and soon after soared to £14,000.

Our own "wheels" came when Barrie bought a 1934 Chevrolet ute. We spent a considerable amount of time improving it. I learnt how to "counter sink" a screw (or a hundred) as we installed a new wooden-tray back floor and we put new perspex blinds on the doors because there were no side windows with the soft cabin roof. Barrie didn't have a licence at this stage, so I drove until that was rectified.

In 1953 Barrie did his six months of Compulsory National Service Training (Nashos) in the Air Force at Amberley. He gained a lot from the experience and thought it would be beneficial for all young men to have a similar opportunity. In between a rigid routine of physical training he was employed in the Drawing Office. He said the instructors were tough but fair, and he came out very physically fit. Barrie became friendly with Doug Aird, a Woombye lad who had a little Morris ute, and they visited the farm to see Mirie and me. One night when returning to Amberley they came across a body on the road as the result of a motorbike accident and had to give evidence in court. But usually their visits were simply good fun.

Barrie and I announced our engagement in the *Queensland Times* newspaper on January 28, 1954. Barrie asked Dad for my hand in marriage, the expected practice in those days. Dad gave permission, so we took a day off work and travelled to Brisbane by train to buy the engagement ring from Wallace Bishop. I wore a white dress (self-made) that acquired quite a few black smudges from the old coal train smut – a normal hazard of rail travel in the '50s and even into the '70s. We could have bought the ring at Hastings in Ipswich, but a trip to Brisbane, despite the coal dust, was a big event and desirable for such a momentous occasion. It was the "done thing" and included lunch at a city restaurant. The solitaire diamond ring cost £40 ($80), which took about a year to save. Those better off spent about £60 or £70, but that was beyond our means. One way of making ends meet and save for the wedding was to go to Aratula or Kalbar at weekends and pick spuds. Barrie and I did a bit of that and I can tell you picking up potatoes is not an easy way to make money.

On a more glamourous note, Barrie and I went to Brisbane to see Queen Elizabeth II when she visited Brisbane in March 1954. We waited for several hours in the grounds of the Booroodabin Bowls Club where my sister, Margaret, and her husband, Keith, were members. We were eventually rewarded when the Queen and the cavalcade passed by on their way from the Brisbane Airport. Later that night we went into the city and waited in the street to watch the royal party go by a second time on their way to a ball held in their honour. We were (and I still am) Royalists and enjoyed our day. We were struck that night by the beauty in the face of our monarch as she was driven by.

My introduction to the Patrick family and their house at 20 Pommer Street widened my knowledge and experience. I discovered that the rule of being seen but not heard did not apply, but of course they only had two kids. If our Harsant family had all started to speak at once it would have been bedlam! Cooking was a big thing on a Sunday morning for Barrie's mum, Eva, and her mother, Annie Hughes, who I called Nana. While the lunch was roasting, cakes, tarts and scones were on the go for the evening meal – tea, as it was called in those days. Cooking everything at the same time saved on wood. The mother-and-daughter team set great store by their baking and were very good at it. This skill reflected Nana's English upbringing. (Barrie's brother, Don, would inherit this culinary skill and love of the kitchen. I wouldn't be able to say the same for Barrie.)

Butter was too expensive for a lot of townies. Until I visited Pommer Street I'd never tasted margarine. It took a while to acquire a taste for it on sandwiches, and even cakes made with marg tasted different to me. Their evening tea, or dinner as we call it now, was served early. On the farm we often didn't get in from the dairy until dark, but in Brassall the meal was on the table by 5.30pm whatever the season to suit the men's working hours and their bus timetables.

I will deviate from the story of my romance with Barrie to fill in his side of the family story. Barrie's father, Ern, worked at the *QT* for about 44 years and was editor for nine of those. Barrie's mother, Eva, would not only become my mother-in-law, but also my best friend.

Eva was born in Crewe, Cheshire, England on April 29, 1910. As a five-month-old she sailed from London to Australia on the *Norseman* with her parents, William and Annie Hughes. They paid £25 to travel third-class steerage. (I still have their ticket, or what remains of it, after 104 years.) Their destination was Brisbane, via Sydney. I never heard how they reached their final destination of Brassall, but perhaps they chose to join others of the Crank family who'd already settled in North Ipswich. Annie was one of Richard Crank and Jessie Eliza Wannell's 14 children.

In April 1912, Eva's parents bought the large Pommer Street block of land from Eva Elizabeth Keidge, who owned several acres in Brassall even before streets were formed. At first they lived in a tent and "humpy" – a huge shock to the system after the busy streets of Crewe. The old Pommy settlers were a pretty stoic lot and there were a number of them settled in the Australian bush of the same Brassall street.

Thanks to a "Workers' Dwellings" loan, their house was finally built in 1928. Annie Hughes's Melbourne Cup sweep winnings provided the deposit. She and a neighbour decided to enter the sweep and, as agreed, Annie bought the ticket. When she asked the other lady for her contribution the woman cried poor and said she couldn't afford to spend money on gambling, leaving Annie to wear it. When Annie's ticket won first prize the neighbour came over wanting to contribute to the purchase of the ticket and share in the spoils of £20. Annie declined and used her winnings as a deposit for their longed-for house.

According to their payment book, Annie and William Hughes were advanced £221 with a monthly repayment of £1/9/3. The payments reflect the value of the currency of the day. There is a note in the Borrowers Passbook saying if the book was lost, a fee of one shilling would be charged for a new book. (Every threepence counted!) In fact, they paid £1/10/- most months, ninepence more than the required amount. William Hughes did not keep in good health and Annie walked from Pommer Street into Ipswich to do laundry work. In February 1932 they made a final lump-sum payment, paying it off more quickly than necessary. They must have saved hard to achieve this result. William Hughes would die only three months later.

Eva Hughes, their daughter, married William Ernest Henry (Ern) Patrick on June 18, 1932 in the Albert Street Methodist Church in Brisbane. Eva worked in the Ipswich Woollen Mills as a "mender". She had a Degree in Music for violin-playing and had achieved Honours in all her music exams, which earned her the right to append the letters ALCM in 1928, an admirable achievement. (Her photo in cap and gown adorns my lounge-room wall to this day.) She married the same day the Battle of Brisbane rugby league Test match took place when Great Britain defeated Australia. Ern always joked that he was sorry to have missed it. I think the marriage was the better option – Eva was a most amazing woman, musically talented and the life of any party. She played the violin right through to her senior years and played in The Key Notes, a band, with Barrie's brother, Don. Eva had hobbies too – cake decorating, hat-making and growing orchids, at all of which she was very proficient.

Barrie was born in 1934 and Don in 1937.

Eva could dance all night. She sang Gracie Fields's songs with great feeling and humour and was a member of the Brassall CWA choir. She was an elegant partner for Ern, who was patron of many sporting clubs and was a great supporter of anything Ipswich or sporting. Because of Ern's occupation as journalist, sub-editor, and then editor of the *QT*, he was the recipient of many invitations, and Eva attended many functions. She loved nice clothes and jewellery and always looked elegant, even when going shopping. She adhered to the notion that "a lady always shops in hat and gloves".

Actually the whole family dressed well. I had a reminder of this one night when Barrie and his mother were acting the fool coming down the steps of the Ipswich Town Hall. Eva fell and broke her right wrist and I offered to do the ironing. In making such a magnanimous gesture I must have been trying to get on Eva's good side. Ern, Barrie and Don were all office workers and all wore long-sleeved cotton shirts, usually white or pastel coloured with collars. There were about 25 shirts to be ironed for the week.

Lori, Kath and Mirie.

Barrie and George Keidge in fancy dress.

Chapter 8

Tying the Knot

Barrie and I were married at St George's Church of England, Waterworks Road, Brassall on October 1, 1955. It was a hot and humid day and sweat ran down my back as I stood at the altar. Our reception was held in the hall across the road from the church. My sister Mirie was my bridesmaid and Don, Barrie's brother, was best man. We wore three-quarter-length frocks, mine a white embroidered nylon, and Mirie's a pale-pink nylon seersucker.

Barrie was still doing a grease and oil change on the old Chev an hour before the wedding. Jim Willmott from the Harrisville garage drove Dad and I to the church from the farm. Dad's effort in giving me away was testament to his strength – he was not long out of hospital after a big stomach operation. I would have postponed my wedding if he could not have made it. He HAD to give me away. Our driver made me jumpy by slowing down on the way. "The bride is always late," he claimed.

As we were about to walk up the aisle Dad insisted on walking on my right side, saying, "Keep the sword arm free!" His right hand being free to use the sword, in case he needed to "jump to the defence".

Dad had a bit of experience as Father-of-the-Bride. I was the fourth daughter to marry. Barbara was the first of us to have a big wedding and had a three-tier wedding cake. One of our neighbours, not to be outdone, made a four-tier cake for her daughter's wedding. Our Margaret, who worked in the Commonwealth Bank in Brisbane, was about to marry Keith Trail, so the lady making her cake went one better and made a five-tier cake. It was a magnificent production, and caused a bit of amusement at the time. After the reception, Kath's husband, George, was carrying the top tier of the cake down the high steps of the Warrill View Hall where the wedding breakfast was held, with his young son, Jimmy, on one arm and dropped the cake. It was said at the time that the icing was so strong it survived the fall with nary a broken piece on arrival at the bottom step. My cake had only three tiers, but was very nice. Mrs Christenson and her mother, Mrs Jackson of Wilsons Plains, baked and iced the cakes for the Harsant weddings. They were wonderful cooks.

Mum, whom Dad described as a "resourceful little woman", catered for Barbara's and Margaret's weddings, no mean effort, with the help of local ladies to wait on the tables. She was a hard worker and did most of the wedding cooking at home with the help of the relevant brides – hams, chickens, salads and trifles. Fortunately, by that time we had the big refrigerator in the dairy and could keep the goodies there.

The bride always wore a special "going-away" outfit and mine was a crushed strawberry two-piece. Barrie had two suits made at Frey and Jacks, tailors in Ipswich, a dark one for the wedding and the other grey with two pairs of strides for a going-away suit. As we were so short of cash I wonder now at the need for that expenditure, but didn't think it unusual in 1955. Since Barrie was a white-collar worker and people dressed more formally in those days, the suits would come in handy after the wedding. No respectable office worker went to work without a tie and a nicely ironed shirt. In all the time I knew Barrie he never went out without a comb in his pocket, and two clean hankies. (In later years he would say he had a clean hankie and a "snot" rag. He liked to shock.) Barrie insisted also that his shoes were polished to the shiniest shine and would sit on the back steps and make sure they were polished every day, ready for work the next morning. Flat heels or Cuban. (He never gave up the habit, especially when R.M. Williams boots were his footwear of choice.) Barrie nearly always wore a hat – a felt type you see in all the old pictures of the '50s, especially in gangster movies or on newspaper reporters and detectives. (In later years he wore a Stetson or the Akubra, turned up at the back, in contrast to the "sheep cockie" style worn turned down all round.)

Barrie and I had our "first night" at Marg and Keith Trail's home in Mayne Junction, Brisbane. As we set off for Noosa Heads the next day it was blowing a dusty gale. It was quite a trip in the old 1934 Chevrolet with the perspex blinds and a big, portable, Bakelite radio on the seat between us, wired up to the car, and going better on the crests of hills. The radio I mean – the ute went better downhill. The smell of the old ute's oil fumes is still in my nostrils today, in my imagination. In 1955 the trip to Noosa was different from today's travel. The motorway, as it is now, wasn't built and travellers passed through most of the small towns along the way, on indifferent road surfaces, mostly one lane each way. Motorists often stopped halfway through the journey for refreshments and petrol, and the driver usually had a "cup of tea and a lie-down" (don't know about the Bex!) upon arrival at their destination, while the lady of the house did the unpacking. Bypassing all the small towns these days with four to six-lane highways makes for a much faster trip.

After travelling about three hours we arrived at Thatcher's, in Hastings Street, Noosa's most modern flats. Still a very sandy main street, with a strip of bitumen down the centre, Noosa hadn't been "discovered". (It amazes me now how easy it was then to rent a place in Hastings Street. I can't afford to shop there these days!)

Graham and Val Kathage, who had married a week before us, occupied the honeymoon flat above. Barrie and Graham were old fishing mates from childhood, both families going to

Noosa Heads for their holidays. Seeing them at Thatcher's was a surprise. Barrie bumped the ceiling in our flat with a fishing rod and called out, "Get yer trousers on, yer bastard, and come fishing".

The four of us did a lot of fishing on our honeymoon, going out in a hired motorboat and spending a lot of time on the beach, swimming or surf fishing for tailor. Dining out was a luxury we could not afford and counter meals didn't exist as far as I know, so I did all the cooking. Graham, being a coal miner, had a more superior set of wheels than ours – even though we had tried to tart our old girl up a bit. We did a few local day trips in his luxurious Vanguard sedan.

Near the end of our two-week honeymoon, Graham, Val, Barrie and I decided to try fishing for tailor at Alexandria Bay so set off on foot in the late afternoon with our four very long surf rods, pilchards for bait, a blanket each and some drinking water. The fishing was a bit slow so we decided to sleep there and get the early morning tide when the fish might be biting. We put a blanket on the sand and all lay on it with the other three blankets on top of us, as it was a cold night. Barrie and I kept waking up thirsty, and when Val and Graham woke up about 2am there was practically no water left and little crabs were getting in our swag. That was it – blow the fishing! We decided to head back to Noosa Heads and our warm beds.

What a circus trying to find our way through the bush in the dark – someone knew of a short cut. Ha! Ha! Long surf rods getting caught in the trees, tripping over shrubs and roots and all that. We eventually found a track and I said, "My dad always says if you see a track in the bush it will lead you somewhere". We followed this advice and eventually came out of the bush right on to the rocky path and precipice over the ocean. The few miles back to Thatcher's was then an easy walk. That was the night I started to get glandular fever. On the way back to the flat we rested on a few big rocks and I found a 10-shilling note ($1) in my coat pocket. It was a godsend. We were all but out of money and still had to get back to Ipswich in the old Chev, a real gas-guzzler.

My first introduction to the delights of Noosa Heads came prior to the honeymoon circa 1952 when I holidayed there with Barrie and the family. It was their favourite holiday haunt. We caught a taxi about 4.30am to the Ipswich Railway Station and started the long trip to Cooroy by train, before getting into an old bus for the last leg of the journey to Noosa Heads. It was always a highlight of the trip to have a platform snack about Caboolture, and return the thick white china cups at the next station. But the best part was the first spectacular glimpse of the ocean, from the top of the Cooroy-Noosa range.

We were encumbered with the things most people going to Noosa in the early '50s deemed essential for the three-week holiday. This included a suitcase, called a port in those days, full of tinned food. Food was expensive at the coast and to augment our fish diet we had an occasional meal of tinned stew, soup or similar with bread. Hardly any food was bought in Noosa for the duration of the holiday, although a bus trip to Nambour was essential for fresh bread and cream-buns. That was where you found the best bakery items. The Patricks's luggage included the compulsory large 7lb. syrup tin of mullet-gut bait that Ern "brewed" for weeks in advance, usually carried in the big creel. Then of course there were the fishing rods, all one piece Rangoon cane, including a couple of long surf rods, plus the reels and tackle so it was a pretty cumbersome, but essential, amount of luggage. The change of trains on Roma Street Station in Brisbane must have required a bit of organisation. I wonder now how the contingent managed when Ern finally bought an Austin A30. Surely they must have transported the long surf rods by some other means or they might have been tied to the top of the car. The rods were probably longer than the little old A30. Father's (Ern's) often-used saying, "The little car went well again" was heard by all and sundry. Eva referred to Ern as Father, and after we married, I followed suit.

Noosa fishing was unsurpassed. Every day we went fishing in an open wooden "putt-putt" boat as they call them now, with an inboard motor, hired from our great friend Len Ely, who owned O-Boats. The motors were "Olds", made in

Maryborough, and very reliable. We stayed out for hours every day, and most days we caught about 60 or 70 fish, mainly bream, and practically lived on fish. In those days, fish were always on the bite, regardless of the state of the tide. Under the tutelage of the Patricks, I became pretty adept at filleting. We often gave our excess fish to campers and other folk around the place. Of course we pumped for yabbies before we cast a line. It was a very busy holiday. Surfing was fitted in between our daily pilgrimages, after the fishing and filleting. Nana, Barrie's grandma, always went out in the boat with us. Getting her off the boat into the bushes and dunes on the bank for toileting was a bit of an effort. Dear old Nana.

The Patricks' Noosa holiday was like a religion to them. It usually featured in a few stories in the *QT* after Ern returned to work. A lot of Ipswichians holidayed there in those days. I remember one of their fishing mates was Dave Colbourne, an Ipswich dentist, the grandfather, we found out years later, of Tracy Wickham, the great swimmer. With all the free publicity he gave the place, Ern was a great advocate for Noosa Heads.

There was always a nightly concert at Laguna House, a popular boarding house about halfway down Hastings Street. Ern and Barrie did a few numbers, with Barrie doing a bit of role acting to suit the song. The Massauds, fishing legends of Noosa Heads and Noosaville, had some great tenors in their family and one or two of them gave a rendition – always including "Pedro the Fisherman". Ern's favourite was "Galway Bay", the words altered to Laguna Bay after Noosa's popular beach. "The Gendarmes", the music-hall classic, was also a favourite of his and Barrie's, along with "Davy Crockett", with props. Some of the houses we stayed in were pretty rickety, with a shower under the tank-stand, saggy beds and cupboards with doors falling off, but very enjoyable all the same. At least we were just about on the surf, and the sound of breakers at bedtime was very soothing.

This love of Noosa Heads was the reason we spent our honeymoon there. The little old beach resort has changed mightily since then. I suppose you could call the Patricks the pioneer holidaymakers in the area. I don't know when they first made Noosa their most desired holiday spot, but in 1932, before they were married, Eva and Ern joined what seemed like half the Brassall and North Ipswich population in holidaying during the Christmas break at Southport or Coolangatta.

Lori on her wedding day with her parents, Jessie and Radford Harsant.

Honeymooners at Noosa.

CHAPTER 9

Head West Young Man

Our first marital home was a flatette rented from Mrs Archibald in Liverpool Street, North Ipswich. It was a closed-in veranda with a sort of wooden slat blind for the external wall and enough room for a gas stove, kerosene refrigerator, a table and two chairs and a dresser in the kitchen. A double bed, wardrobe and duchess, with enough room to walk down the side of the bed, was our boudoir. Bathing was managed under the house near the laundry in an unpainted galvanised iron bath on legs. We didn't have a washing machine. Water was boiled in a "copper" for a hot bath. Barrie was chopping chips for the copper to do the washing one day and he just about cut off a finger, which meant a quick trip to the hospital for stitches.

On our return from our honeymoon, I discovered, after a visit to our humble abode by Dr. Garozzo, I had a severe case of glandular fever. I felt like a poor relation and somewhat embarrassed with our humble home, but our place was all we could afford and, even though I had wonderful in-laws, it was better than living with rellies. Barrie did the washing while I was sick, and when I looked out at the line I saw a string of hankies all pegged up like you would hang out towels. He never had to help with the laundry again in our 47 years of marriage. Even pegs were an item used sparingly, and I hung the clothes up much differently from how I do now. Every penny counted when we were married.

Mrs Archibald gave us both some good advice when we went to live in her flat. "Don't go to sleep on an argument – sort it out before you go to bed," she said. Privately to me she said, "Never turn down a chance to go out with hubby when he asks. He might get used to it and stop asking". This proved costly when I was a new bride. One Sunday I had a rolled roast beef cooking in the oven when Barrie asked me to go for a drive. I switched off the gas, leaving the meat in the oven. Upon our return I finished the cooking, set the table and started to carve the roast. After removing the top layer of delicious-looking beef I was shocked to see dozens of heads waving to me. It was maggots. It turned us off our lunch of course, and was consigned to the rubbish bin. (A new bride never stops learning!) Looking back now on those days when we were first married, I realise how immature, innocent and inexperienced I was as a 20-year-old, especially compared to the young ladies of today. I suppose our parents thought we were pretty worldly in our outlook. When we became engaged and married we spent our time almost exclusively with each other or family. We never went out "with the girls" or "with the mates", which seems to be the normal way of life these days, and a good thing too, I think, in moderation.

By the time we were married Barrie had left the paper and was working as Head Storeman at Woolworths in Brisbane Street. The Woolies staff gave us a cocktail tray for a wedding present, which is still in the cupboard somewhere. I can't remember what the *QT* gave us. I went back to my job at the *QT,* which was unusual for a married woman, but I enjoyed working there. (One lasting memory is the smell of newsprint ink and my dirty clothes and hands from handling newspapers.)

When we were married, Barrie was earning about £11 a week (having a rise of 2/- that month). I also had a rise of 1/6d to bring me up to about £7. Wages had been frozen for a couple of years, so in retrospect it was a fairly paltry raise. As this was before the influx of cheap imported clothing we had to save for quite a while to get anything new. On discovering "time payment" I had bought and paid off my Singer sewing machine when I first started work in Ipswich. The same for my first wristwatch. In later years I recall my father saying that the way cheap things were being brought into the country our manufacturers would soon be out of business. I don't think he was too far out in his prediction.

The *QT*'s Annual Christmas Party, held at the Croquet Club in Queens Park, was a highlight. Some staff, usually those from the office and editorial departments, put on some entertainment. Barrie and his father sang a song or two, with actions and costumes pertaining to the song, a repertoire similar to that of our Noosa holidays. Father also recited "The One Eyed Yellow Idol", which he liked to do at the drop of a hat. The staff produced a little paper called *Cutie* with members of the staff being the butt of some jokes and poems. It always caused a great deal of amusement.

After some time at Woolworths, Barrie decided to take on a pie run, working for "Reeves Pies". He bought an Austin A40 utility, it being more economical to run than the Chev. The hot-pie system was much the same as now I think – a box on the back of the ute with an old chip heater to keep the pies hot. Always the joker, Barrie went around the streets ringing a bell and calling out, "Hot pies, full of flies, maggots in the corners". The clientele was mostly female and Barrie enjoyed sharing jokes. The weather was a reliable topic of conversation, particularly if it was a good day for washing.

The pie run proved a hand-to-mouth existence, but we were never short of leftover pies to eat! It was at this time we started thinking we might "head West". We almost went to Tallegalla near Ipswich to work on a dairy farm, but after consulting my father, sanity prevailed and we gave it a miss.

Barrie then decided he wanted to work for the Department of Agriculture and Stock as a Stock Inspector. Barbara's husband, Bob Hunter, worked in the department as a Dairy Officer and gave Barrie some advice on how to go about it. Barrie started to study by correspondence for entrance. A bit hard after a long day's work.

Bob and Barbara lived at Southport at that time, with one or two children, and we sometimes spent weekends with them, a great change of scenery. We girls sometimes talked Bob into taking us for a picnic on the Broadwater at Southport, but I don't think Bob was ever completely enthusiastic. He said picnics meant flies, ants or sand in the sandwiches. Bob had been injured in World War II, which bothered him somewhat, but he soldiered on and was a wonderful husband, father and friend. Barrie had a lot of faith in his advice and always enjoyed his company and wisdom. We always dreamt of success and didn't want to be the poor relations for ever. (It would be a sad day when Bob died, too young, in December 1972.)

In early 1957 we went to Brisbane and did the rounds of the stock and station agents looking for work on the land, but with no success. A bit deflated, we decided to advertise for work in the *Queensland Country Life* newspaper, looking for station hand and governess positions. Grammar-school-educated, we noted in the ad. We struck it lucky. One of the readers on a sheep station called Culladar needed both a ringer (station hand) and governess. They decided to give a married couple a go, and Mrs Margaret Clark-Dickson, who was spending a short time in the city, requested our attendance at an interview in Hamilton Heights in Brisbane. We passed muster and excitedly prepared for our new adventure. Barrie had no experience with sheep, but could ride a horse and had done cattle work with us on the farm. He'd also done casual herd recording for the Ag. and Stock Department on dairy farms around the Gold Coast Hinterland. I had no experience as a governess, but had enough education to supervise the Correspondence School lessons that would arrive by weekly mail. What we both had was plenty of enthusiasm.

Barrie *had* to equip himself with a .303 sporting rifle, a must for a prospective ringer, and by the time we paid for that and our train fares (to be refunded) we were just about skint. We turned up at Roma Street Station with a tin trunk and some ports, (portmanteaux as Dad would say) and of course the .303. We had our own blankets and bed linen in addition to our clothes, and of course my piano-accordion, so it was hard to cut down on our gear. The Railways asked us for a fair bit of money for excess luggage and we were fortunate that Nana Hughes, who'd come to see us off, came good with a loan. There were many tears from my in-laws on the platform before our departure, but we were so happy and excited we didn't feel much sympathy for those left behind. We also left the Austin A40 behind to be sold. There was no trouble about carrying the rifle in the train. I think the bolt had to be removed.

After a day sitting on the bank of the Fitzroy River in Rockhampton waiting for our connection to Chorregon siding between Longreach and Winton, we were again on the move. We went easy on spending on food and luckily the railway refreshment rooms en route had cheap tea and sandwiches. We felt secure in the thought that from here on we'd be making money, not paying rent or buying food, and looked forward to saving for the first time in our lives. When the train conductor offered us a sleeper for 10 bob ($1 today), we took it.

For some, the vast, empty vista may have dulled their enthusiasm. Not us. The landscape of Western Queensland's wide-open spaces as seen from the train window attracted us both and we felt happy and excited in the change of direction our lives were taking. Anyway, we didn't have the money to go back and wanted our fares refunded as part of the deal. We landed at our destination with £1 ($2) to our names, but with a determination to begin on our road to success, fame and fortune. My weekly salary was £5 ($10) and Barrie's £11, all found, meaning food and accommodation was provided.

As we might go three months before getting to the shops, we considered ourselves on a good wicket.

When we finally arrived at Chorregon siding, the boss, Don Clark-Dickson, met us in his big Ford sedan. Thanks to a wool boom a few years earlier, most graziers had good, large cars in those days. When Don commented on our large amount of luggage I replied, "Shows we're not here for a fortnight".

As our train headed west towards Winton and we were leaving the siding, our boss let out an oath. Lo and behold the countryside was on fire. Our coal-burning train had ignited a grassfire. We had a wild ride to Culladar, opening several gates on the way. The boss immediately got into a fire truck, which was always ready to go in the fire season with watertank filled and fire-fighting gear on board. He headed off, declining Barrie's offer to go with him, and we reacquainted ourselves with Mrs Dickson. (We dropped the *Clark* in our reference to the lovely lady.) After I'd been introduced to Denise, Deborah and little pre-schooler Lindy (Belinda) – the children, my charges – we inspected our cottage and were shown where to go for our meals.

In one of the stories Barrie wrote about his time at Culladar, he described Mrs Dickson thus:

> *The chastity of a nun, the bearing of an attractive star, coupled with a magnetic personality and a heart of gold. To put it in the words of an old rogue bushman, Jack Tennant, who when in his cups looked up from the dinner table, face-to-face with her for the first time, after receiving his meal – "My God, what an impressive-looking woman".*

We'd never been away from south-east Queensland before and the atmosphere, smells and feeling of freedom were new. There'd been a good season here and the grass was thick and long.

There would be many grass fires during our stay on Culladar and Barrie would do his fair share of fire-fighting. On one occasion the flames came right up to the house yard, but a fortuitous wind change and a bit of watering prevented damage to the homestead. One day there were about seven fires around us and 10 trucks with two-man crews, all from neighbouring stations, on the job. Most of the fires were started by lightning strikes. Barrie said the worst fire-fighting incident was when the boss was driving and he was on the back of the truck with the hose, and lightning struck mere inches away. The rubber tyres on the truck saved the men from electrocution.

After one fire, hundreds of dead and dying sheep piled up on a fenceline where they became trapped. Barrie and Don shot those still showing some sign of life. Some of the "dead wool" was taken off the animals and sold. It was a fairly major disaster. I wouldn't have liked the job of getting the wool off. Of course on a sheep station, or any station for that matter, there are always unpleasant chores.

I took photographs on our old Box Brownie. I'd climb the watertank tower to see where the fires were and relay the information to Mrs Dickson, who was constantly on the phone to neighbours advising where the trucks were needed. Sometimes after a big fire was extinguished, the men from several stations gathered around the house tankstand drinking rum, courtesy of Don. Fire ploughing – going around the perimeter of the property ploughing close to the fences and roads – was undertaken in the hope the ploughed section would stop a grassfire at that juncture. Schoolwork was inevitably held up a little during the fire-fighting season.

At some stage the boss decided we should have our residence renovated from a one-room, two-veranda abode to become a self-contained cottage with kitchenette, shower and toilet. Indoor septic if you please. One reason for the renovation was to relieve Mrs Dickson of the chore of cooking for the staff. In August 1957, Tom Spence, a popular builder in the West was given the job. I was knitting Barrie a maroon turtle-necked jumper at the time and said to Tom, "I bet I'll finish this jumper before you finish the cottage". I only just did.

The renovations were completed in four weeks. Luxurious! Once the reno was complete and we had our new kitchen, we bought and cooked our own food and our pay went up to compensate.

Electricity on the station came from a wind-lite, a wind-driven mechanism like a windmill, connected to batteries with an engine in the event of insufficient wind. The electrical 32-volt wiring was done by a mate of ours, Graham Palmer, another Ipswichian who had done an electrical apprenticeship in the Ipswich Railway Workshops, but now worked on a nearby station. Barrie knew him from school days when Graham's family lived in North Ipswich. Like Barrie, Graham wanted to venture into the wild west.

We had the new septic tank a few weeks when it became obvious it wasn't working properly, in other words it was leaking. When we first went to Culladar our toilet was an old corrugated-iron edifice about 100 yards from our cottage. A "long drop" with *two* seats. This amused me, but we never did visit simultaneously. It faced west, so you could enjoy some nice sunsets if you happened to be there at the right time. One didn't close the door as there wasn't another building in that direction for at least 10 miles, although "a sheep or two and a kangaroo", even some wild pigs, might appear while one was sitting and ruminating.

It was decided that the new septic tank would need to be cleaned out and replastered with concrete. Who had to go down the hole? The ringer of course. Barrie Patrick.

The hole at the top of the tank was about 18" x 18" (about 45 cm) and I think it must have been about eight feet deep (about 240 cm). I felt sorry for Barrie. It would have been most unpleasant down there – steamy, hot and malodorous. And it was summer, which made it worse. A nasty job. *Undeterred*, my ringer manfully struggled on. He passed up buckets full of matter by way of someone on top with a rope to pull said bucket to the surface until the tank was empty. Washing the surface with clean water followed. He then plastered the surfaces with cement passed down by the old bucket until all was done. After a few days it was dry enough for a trial. Fortunately it was successful. "If you do a job, do it properly" was Barrie's adage and we were soon back to "doing it" in the house. Barrie also said, "The greater the adversity, the sweeter the success". It is a pretty apt saying, especially regarding septic tanks, but I am not sure about "sweetness" in this instance. Barrie said he missed the old dunny at first because he did his best thinking there at night, looking at the western skies and myriad stars.

I was a new bride with little experience – except that gained under Mum's and Eva's eyes – and we missed Mrs Dickson's wonderful cooking. Eventually my kitchen skills improved slightly, although my scone-making ability remained poor. Once Mrs Dickson went to be with a very ill relative in Brisbane at a moment's notice and I was asked to do the cooking at the homestead. We'd run out of bread and the weekly delivery (with the mail) was still a day or two away, so I made scones for lunch. There was no self-raising flour available, but I found a recipe using plain flour. Instead of then using a teaspoon of baking powder, I put in a tablespoon, with less than desirable results. At the time, Lindy was very young and the boss wouldn't let her eat one in case she got sick.

Mrs Dickson taught me a lot about cooking, especially mutton, our only meat supply. Barrie, the ringer, had to kill a sheep (a "killer") every few days on dusk and hang it in the "Butcher Shop" overnight to be cut into joints early the next day. It was then shared between the two kitchens. In recent times I heard a fellow being interviewed about sheep on ABC Radio. He said, "You can't eat Merinos". I beg to differ – we ate Merino hoggets for about 15 years of our married life. I have an old mutton recipe book called *Once a Jolly Jumbuck*, illustrated by Mrs Dickson, and the first recipe is "To Prepare Brains before Cooking". The last recipe is "Real Scotch Haggis".

After a kill, wedgetail eagles and kite hawks hovered, looking for titbits. At night offal fires were lit and Barrie and I often sat in the dark waiting for foxes to come up to where the remains were burning. As soon as he spotted the eyes in the firelight, Barrie would take a shot with the .303. We rejoiced if he succeeded because they caused devastation among a mob of ewes with lambs at foot. Poor lambs – the foxes always went for the eyes and it was heartbreaking to see them if they survived an attack. Eagles too were the enemy of the lambs and Barrie shot a couple of huge specimens. Graham the electrician enjoyed a bit of "huntin' and shootin'" and he and Barrie spent many a weekend chasing 'roos and pigs. The damage the pigs and foxes caused the lambs meant the fellas had no compunction in shooting them. After the pigs were found, usually in a gully, they took off at the first sign of a human and the chase was on. At times the huntsmen ran for miles. The bounty on foxes and pig snouts paid by the council in Longreach was welcome – it added a few more shillings to our hoped-for wealth.

One of Barrie's jobs was to milk the goats. Luckily he'd learnt a bit about milking when courting me on the dairy farm. I never liked cows' milk on the farm, but I took a real liking to goats' milk. Cool on a hot day, it was a delicious luxury.

The weekly mail truck, driven by one Don Blunt (by name and nature), was a highlight. Don arrived at Culladar on the second day of the run out of Longreach, carrying everything from mail, building materials, hardware and groceries, including butter, fruit and vegetables. The grocer in Longreach wrapped the butter in hessian and the mailman placed it in an area of the truck under the tabletop, usually reserved for tools and ropes. Don watered it at every stop to keep it damp and cool. The wet bags and the cool breeze ensured its edible condition on arrival. The summer heat, up to 50 degrees Centigrade, was a good test for the wet-bag cooling system. Except for bananas, all food arrived in reasonable condition. Although once the neighbour's dogs got hold of the butter before it made it to our place. Don threw the cartons and mailbags down from the top of the load to whoever was on the ground waiting to catch them, regardless of gender or age. Bad luck if you missed. Don then came in and had smoko, a cuppa and a piece of cake or a Sao biscuit with Vegemite before going on his way.

School was conducted in a special room enclosed with flyscreen mesh at the end of one of the homestead verandas. Barrie and I, and a casual worker at times, ate our meals on that veranda near the kitchen before we had our own kitchen. We kept pretty regular school hours and the children were taught using the Correspondence School lessons, a very good educational tool delivered by the mail truck. Ironically, when I was nine or 10 years old, my Uncle Eric Payne, who worked as Senior Clerk in the Literary Assistance Branch of the Queensland Education Department, came with a film crew to our farm at Radford to make a movie about the Correspondence School called *Mail Way*. The younger Harsant kids played parts and some of us, Barb in particular, stood in for the professional actors, riding horses and mustering. Our Uncle Cedric also put on clothes the same as the actors and did some horse scenes. Some of us went to Brisbane to watch the film in a theatre when it opened. It was a real eye-opener for us country kids, but never did I think I would one day be acting out the same scenes in real life, except I was now the teacher.

My job at Culladar was to see that the work set by the teachers in Brisbane was completed and returned on the next weekly mail-out. After school we sometimes rode around the station, but otherwise there was little extracurricular activity. At one stage I made some clothes for the girls on Mrs Dickson's sewing machine.

Once when the dam near the house was nearly empty, the boss suggested we take some wire netting and catch some fish, the progeny of some he had put in earlier. Barrie and I got into the mucky water, clothed, and dragged in quite a good haul. We cooked them, quite excited about the prospect of a change of diet, as fish was hard to come by in the West, until we began to eat. They were full of bones. In fact they were bony bream and inedible. All that effort!! At least the netting lark cooled us down and provided a diversion. Owing to the distance from a hairdresser, I adopted a new hairstyle at Culladar. When my hair was long enough, I changed to wearing a chignon (bun). I enjoyed that look and the fishing in the muddy dam didn't affect my hair too much. I have a photo of that day to prove it, although the wet dress hanging around my legs didn't look too glamorous.

Not long after we went to Culladar, Barrie's father had a heart attack. This was an enormous worry for us. We felt we should have been there for Eva, but time and distance made it impossible. (We would have many more occasions in the future when we wished we were closer to our families. But we chose our lifestyle and had to make the best of being far from loved ones.) To our relief, Father made a good recovery. He even managed a holiday with us, which supplied him with plenty of material for his pen.

Father was at Culladar during the August shearing. At one stage the daytime temperature reached 42 degrees Celsius. This quite surprised him. Even then there was a great variance in the weather – it is not a new phenomenon, just spoken about more these days I suspect.

During our couple of years at Culladar, Barrie improved his riding skills through necessity, riding a couple of broncs that enjoyed a buck or two, in some cases resulting in his coming off as soon as mounting during early morning muster starts. The back boundary of the station was about 10 miles from the homestead and often the men rode that far before coming across a mob of sheep to muster back to the shed and yards for either shearing, crutching or lamb marking. Lunch – usually bread and cold mutton – was carried in a saddlebag. They always carried neck bags with water and a quart pot strapped to the saddle to boil up for a dinner-camp cuppa. Barrie wrote a piece about his battle with his mustering nag, Tambo.

Riding Tambo

It was Monday, and I was up at 3.30a.m., ran the horses in, milked the goats, saddled up and went in for breakfast. We grabbed our lunches – damper with fat and cold mutton – and walked to the horses, silently. I think, all the while, cursing the butter-eating dogs (on the mail run) and a breakdown in the daily bread bit, somewhere along the line.

By this time I reckoned I had this horse by the short hair. I was beginning to enjoy our tussle and knew within myself I had at last hit the front. He'd had a fair spell and looked good. He blew out a bit when I had girthed him in the dark in the yard, but after I kneed him in the guts he relaxed and I took the girth up a bit – just right, I reckoned. The boss had said in passing as he sometimes did with a weather eye, "Have a look after breakfast, he might need a bit more (girthing)". I walked over to the tree under which the horse stood and he turned and looked at me. I don't think I'll ever forget that look or my silent decision. You won't throw me this morning you bastard, and you'll work all day, like me. I slipped the reins off the wire hook on the athel tree, holding them in my cupped fingers as taught, not over a crooked elbow. I slipped my greaseproof and newspaper-wrapped lunch into the saddlebag, and old Psycho went berserk. He put on a glorious exhibition (with no-one in the saddle) that today's TV cameramen would have been proud to present. I hadn't had a chance to buckle the straps on the saddlebag, so during the demo my gourmet lunch flew high into the air and landed without breaking open, with a bit of a flop on the ground. I picked up my lunch, grabbed the rein when I could get close enough to him in the homestead yard, and somehow or other replaced it in the saddlebag and buckled it up. I then gritted my teeth and handed out an order, would you believe, to the boss. "Open up that @@@@ gate, and let me through!" The only words I heard from the boss were "Watch him!" I don't think I remember mounting the bastard, but there we were, the two of us. Rider and horse each with the same determination and I believe, the same hatred for each other. It had to come out and it did.

He put it to me as usual, but I feel with a little more gusto and expertise. He tried to wipe me off against the homestead fence, straight up and straight down. Somehow, I had an elated feeling of newly developed ability and triumph, swearing at him to make it a bit better – up again, down – and then, with all my strength pitted against him as he came down hard again, I pulled the monkey out with the D's and landed on the broad of my back on a small stone. A sharp pain, brief blackness with intermittent stars, and the sight of a 40-foot-high horse continuing with his demonstrative art. The boss caught him. I couldn't fly straight up this time. It took me a while to gain breath and composure, and throw the "monkey" away, which was for a short time still gripped tightly in my hand. I got back up and he had another go, but not as good, thank Christ, and I stayed there with a handful of mane and a seared memory of advice. As we rode away to start work, after a bit of a warm-up, I will never forget the boss's words, "You've got him beat – he's starting to shit". To which I replied, "He only just beat me to it".

About six that night when I let the big bastard go, he sort of half held the bit between his teeth and nearly pulled me over as he bolted for freedom. The boss said, "You want to watch that – I've seen blokes get hurt like that, don't let 'em see too much daylight when you let 'em go. Best to keep them faced up to something". I was lost for words. "Four o'clock should do in the morning," he said, "as long as we're at the yards by daylight we'll be right. No need for a horse."

All I could see, and actually all I had pictured, for the last couple of hours was the glorious sight of a yellow label put on in Bundaberg, and a frosted can. I only used to have one rum in the afternoon those days, and after a hard day. That afternoon I had two real big bastards and two tins of beer, a hot shower and went to sleep with my head on our little cottage's dinner table. Sorry, I forgot to mention that when we pulled up on Dinner Camp that day my damper and fat appeared to be somewhat crushed and crumpled. The mutton, of course, due to cold mutton's consistency remained unscathed. You might say I didn't have to "Break The Bread", but somehow I remember mumbling something like "Give us this day, our daily bread". The butter didn't bear mentioning.

The "Monkey" Barrie mentioned, for those unfamiliar with equine terms, is a strap attached to the saddle with metal "D's". The boss, in his early instructions to his new recruit, said it was inadvisable to grab the monkey, as he had seen fellows hurt that way when the monkey gave way. Barrie rode Tambo from the siding at Chorregon to Culladar in August 1957, a ride of several miles, possibly about as many as 15. He had been railed from Tambo, hence the name. I hopped on the horse when they arrived, to give him a bit of a try-out, and he reefed about a bit, but I didn't think he was that bad. You can never tell. He was probably tired after the trip.

I helped muster on a Sunday a couple of times, ready for a Monday morning start for the shearers, and after mustering cattle all my life, found I had no liking for sheep, the most exasperating animals on earth. Shearing was always done in August. Apparently the shearers didn't like females in the sheds (a bad-luck omen), but I was "allowed" in the shed on one occasion to have a quick look at the goings-on.

Weekends generally started at midday Saturday, which was usual even in a town job, and I am sure the ringers must have relished the chance to have a day and a half relaxation. The single men had to do their washing on the weekends and general personal maintenance. We were lucky that we had the use of the washing machine at the "Big House", which made a big difference – and my ringer had a wife to do *his* laundry!

Our infrequent trips to Longreach or Winton were eagerly anticipated. Sometimes it was three months between excursions to town, often to attend the races, show or campdraft, fitting in a visit to the shops. If it was an overnighter in Longreach, Barrie and I usually stayed at the Welcome Home Hotel; the station owners and managers patronised the bar and lounge of the Commercial.

The ringers called themselves "dungers", knowing they were the lowest of the low in the pecking order in station life and were given the worst chores (whether Grammar School educated or not). As far as the "dungers" were concerned, jackeroos were to be scorned. Jackeroos often ate at the boss's table, wearing a collar and tie, but they were on lower wages than ringers. The fellas would say, "Doing all that money just to eat with the boss!!"

I had my first beer in the lounge of the Commercial – ladies didn't go into the bar in those days. I'm not sure how we "dungers" came to be in the manager's pub. It was probably to prove a point. In later years I wondered why we thought the Commercial was so posh.

On one occasion Barrie was asked to drive the truck, a four-tonner I think, to Longreach to pick up a rainwater tank. It was suggested I go along for a couple of days off. It was the worst trip of my life. It was so hot and the road so rough I thought I'd pass out. The vehicles weren't air-conditioned in 1957 and I kept asking Barrie to stop so I could get a drink from the waterbag hanging under the tray of the truck. I must have been soft in those days. We didn't carry iced water in the '50s. In fact, a bottle of water in the cab soon became too warm to drink. The overnighter at the Welcome Home Hotel was most welcome that night. I had never stayed in a hotel until then, although I was 23 at the time.

We also visited Winton, where Searle's Menswear was the place for the men, and Capel's or Mrs Wooderson's for the ladies. The North Gregory was the best hotel in the West, having been burnt down and replaced more than once over the years. The council owned it and starched white linen and polished silver and glassware were the norm. There was also a large general store in Winton called Corfield and Fitzmaurice ("Corfields" as we referred to it), which sold almost everything.

Sometimes the ringers and wives (if any) would have a get-together such as a barbecue or afternoon tea. I played the piano-accordion for a sing-along. They were held at one or other of our cottages, and we had a really good group of friends. We didn't all have a vehicle and we had to rely on the station management to lend us wheels, usually the station truck.

Our friend, Mike Egan, owned a Ford ute that held four of us in the front seat and on rare occasions we went to town for the pictures. One Saturday, some of us had a trip to Muttaburra in someone's old Land Rover ute where we had lunch at the pub. We all had steak, as beef was an unaccustomed luxury on a sheep station. Food poisoning struck. The next day Graham, the electrician, who hadn't gone to Muttaburra, was wiring the cottage and every time he yelled for Barrie to hand him a tool or piece of equipment Barrie was at the loo. I must have had a more cast-iron stomach, as I was the only steak eater unaffected. The old ringer who ate his wife's T-bone steak, as well as his own, thought his last days had come.

About six months after our arrival at Culladar, the Russian satellite Sputnik circled our planet. Of course we were all out watching the sky for this momentous occasion. Being about 100 miles from the nearest streetlight, we had a great view – the sky was as clear as you would ever see it. The first orbit was on October 4, 1957 and took a bit over one and a half hours to complete a circuit. We often stood out in the night, under the stars, waiting for Sputnik to go overhead.

The local Tower Hill Picnic Races were approaching and Barrie and I prepared Don's horses for competition. We galloped on a cleared track for a few weeks before the big day. "Riding work" I suppose you would call it. I can't recall if there were many wins, but Celeste and Lady Puzzle, Don's best racers, were quite successful. *We* were not eligible to attend the Picnic Races – a ringer was not high enough up the pecking order. A governess was, but naturally I wouldn't attend if it meant leaving Barrie at home.

In retrospect, it amazes me how well Barrie coped with, and accepted, the harshness of being a ringer in the West. After all he'd had a town upbringing (as the son of a newspaper editor) and his main employment had been as a clerk; and he had limited experience with horses and none at all with sheep! He was a stubborn bugger!

The general social norm was: the hierarchy doesn't mix with ringers. Regarding the local Tower Hill Picnic Races, the boss said that we could both go on the proviso that we lunched down by the creek. No thank you. There were lots of ringers in the district – some with wives – who would have swelled the attendance and enhanced the event, had they been allowed.

It was just how it was in those days, although I've been told that the Winton-Longreach area was more snobbish and class-conscious than other sheep areas.

The snobbery of the "Landed Gentry" didn't worry me much, as it takes all kinds to make up the population and there are people I wouldn't be overly keen to share my table with, but as life goes on one becomes more broad-minded about these things and more accepting. As someone once said: *No human being should be considered better than another by the mere accident of birth, but some are more equal than others.* I also noted a saying by Lady someone or other: *Rural society was a small select aristocracy born booted and spurred to ride, and a large dim mass born saddled and bridled to be ridden.*

Barrie later wrote about the snobbery we experienced during our time on Culladar:

> *The privileged did things that we didn't. They used to fart a far, when we went out to fight a fire. They plarnted; we planted. They darnced; we danced. They even cut a few capers in the blacksmith's shop I understand. But there's one thing they didn't do – they didn't fool anybody except themselves. Reality is a great leveller. All of us have to face it in different proportions at times. However, I am of the opinion that it comes much harder to those who think they are above it, yet appear to be less able to cope with it when it strikes unannounced and be inescapably endured. The pendulum swings, the wheel turns. The back country has lost a lot of good men through this so-called class distinction. The class I have yet to get a full and clear description of. The stench of its very initiation and existence will be a blemish on the Australian effort and a blight forever on our heritage. I am a great believer in setting a standard of acceptable behaviour, social morals and sensible laws and the adherence to same. However, I will never accept the pathetic attitude of a section of snob-nosed bastards who seem to think they don't fart as loud as the rest of us. To*

*repeat a saying of an old millionaire friend of mine: The
world is full of heroes; so is the bloody cemetery!*

We couldn't even go to a cricket match, a factor that
ultimately contributed to our leaving the West. Barrie could
play a reasonable standard of cricket as it was part of his school
curriculum. When there was a cricket day coming up at the end
of our second year, the boss said that if it had been up to him
we could go, but "it wasn't the done thing". He said if he made
Barrie an overseer it would be OK but it would seem strange to
others that there was both a manager *and* an overseer on such a
small station. Culladar was 50,000 acres in size, running about
6000 sheep.

Barrie replied, "Don't worry, Don – we won't be here. We'll
head off back to Ippy. I'm going back to the Stock Inspector
studies I gave up to come here".

This was news to me. I was quite content to stay on. I really
loved it and enjoyed my job. Although a bit of a test of my
limited abilities at times, the girls were delightful. I think I did
reasonably well in the supervision of their lessons and having
a lovely person like Margaret Clark-Dickson as a boss was a
bonus. But anyway, we left Culladar in time to get home for
Christmas 1958 and took Johnny, our black kelpie, with us.

The cottage and bathroom at Culladar.

Barrie on Tambo.

CHAPTER **10**

Back to the Big Smoke

We managed a fortnight's holiday at Laguna House at Noosa and watched the Davis Cup for the three days of play at the Milton Tennis Courts. We saved some money to do these extravagant things, but felt that we deserved a bit of luxury after our sojourn in the bush. We also bought a car, a second-hand Austin A40. A few months later, as Barrie was deep into his correspondence studies, we found a largish cheque from Culladar that we had overlooked. It was so overdue for banking that we contacted Don Clark-Dickson to say we were about to put it into our account. I think he was surprised.

Barrie had resumed his study for the Stock and Meat Inspector's exams he dropped when we went west. He thought of studying while working as a ringer, but it proved too tiring, so now he began his full-time slog and I became pregnant.

I didn't work during this time, probably because of being pregnant, but I supported Barrie in his slog. We relied solely on our savings, which eventually paid off with the government job the study earnt him. We never thought to apply for the "dole" or other financial assistance. In fact, there was probably nothing available in our instance. The first government assistance we received was Child Endowment after Steven was born. Barrie achieved good marks in his exams, which he deserved after the hours he put in, sitting at the dining-room table of his parents' home in Pommer Street where he was born and where we spent those six months. I helped around the house and gave the other two ladies in residence, Nana and Eva, a bit of a break. With three generations living together, there was always plenty of washing, ironing and cooking to do. We moved out before the fourth generation arrived.

When Barrie sat on the back steps to take a break from the books, he talked to Billy the budgie, whose cage was on the back landing. By the time the study was finished Billy was quite a good talker. The back landing and steps, in my mind, is the place where you sit and ponder, shine your shoes, keep a budgie, have a yarn, watch the sunsets, have a quiet drink and a smoke (before you saw the error of your ways), watch the moon and the stars, do a bit of canoodling, catch the evening breeze, look at the pot plants and the kangaroos, hares and the birds. Barrie made good use of the back steps while studying for his exams. He was a deep thinker. He also wrote some poems sitting on the back steps. Then there is the back yard where the men go to water the lawn, and feed the dogs, and the ladies go to hang out the washing on the Hills hoist.

In July 1959 Barrie decided to improve things under the house for his mother, and the fact that the new car required garaging hastened things. So a big concrete job was undertaken by the two of us, with a hand-driven cement mixer. Hard work. On the last day, with cement still wet from the final pour, Barrie went to a big football match in Brisbane with his father. It was a Queensland v NSW game, where three Ipswichians, Gary Parcell, Dud Beatty and Noel Kelly, were playing in the front row. A game not to be missed! While they were away the cocker-spaniel dog from next-door inspected the job, leaving his deep footprints all over the site. Being the only one at home, it fell to me to erase the evidence left by Ricky. No easy job, being pregnant! It was very awkward and I made sure the dog was locked up before he could do any more damage.

There was a wait for an appointment with the Department of Ag and Stock, now called the Department of Agriculture, Fisheries and Forestry. We shifted into another little flat, slightly larger than Liverpool Street, only just, but again a side-veranda flat. It was in Cribb Street, near the Blair School. I wanted to be in our own place before the baby was born and we looked for something cheap. We at least had some income from Barrie's various labouring jobs to pay the rent while we waited. On the other side of the wall of our flat were two women friends. One of the ladies, a church organist, practised in their lounge room. We loved the music, which often put us to sleep. (I have fond memories of those days, especially when I hear "How Great Thou Art". I feel I know it intimately.)

Black-and-white television came to Brisbane in August 1959. The in-laws at Pommer Street had a Phillips 14-inch and sometimes we visited and watched in awe. Television! What a wonderful invention! On November 9, we arrived home from a visit and once into bed I felt entirely new sensations. "I think the baby is coming," I said. I got up and made a cuppa while Barrie brought the car around to the back door and hustled me into it. When I arrived at the Ipswich General Hospital (Private) the sister said, "You should have stayed at home and scrubbed floors or something. The baby will be a while arriving".

Steven was born 24 hours later, in the middle of the night, getting into the 10th day of November by 25 minutes. In those days, information on the sex of the baby before birth was not available, so our beautiful boy was a wonderful surprise. We gave our four children one name only, considering that quite sufficient. We thought that a bit radical, but later found a few other people had the same idea.

After 10 days in hospital, I returned to Cribb Street and found the cup of tea I wasn't allowed to drink on the 9th still sitting on the kitchen table. You can imagine what it looked like after 10 days. Barrie was having his meals at his parents' place and hadn't got around to doing any housework.

As we only had an ice chest, I'd take the baby in the stroller up to the nearby butcher daily to get meat for dinner. We lived under the flight path of the Canberra bombers from Amberley and consequently had a very unsettled baby. After a few weeks he settled down as we waited impatiently for the call-up to the Department of Ag. and Stock. We spent Christmas at the farm. A few hints from my mother and Barbara helped greatly, not surprising considering the experience of 12 children between them. After receiving Mum and Barb's advice, Steve became a delight. We visited Barrie's parents and Nana while they holidayed at Burleigh Heads and on March 12, 1960, with Bob and Barb Hunter as godparents, Steven Patrick was baptised at St Peter's Church, Southport.

Our savings were soon depleted, but Barrie found fill-in jobs to keep the wolf from the door. He laboured in many places, including the new Railway Workshops being built at Redbank. Before we went to Culladar, he worked in the Railway Workshops at North Ipswich, cleaning engines, sitting in the barrel of locos, scraping the soot out with a chisel while holding a candle to see. While he was working at Redbank, our mates' father, Jack Egan, came up and spoke to Barrie. Jack, Chief Architect in the Queensland Railways, was inspecting the job. Barrie was digging a trench at the time – bobcats were not in use in those days – so he stopped work, shook hands, rolled a smoke and had a yarn. The other workers were amazed at his temerity. "Big Wigs" never fazed Barrie – he could talk to anyone.

Around June 1960 Barrie was digging trenches at the Qld University at St Lucia when a letter came appointing him to the position of Stock Inspector (Div. 2) at the Toowoomba Stock Office. Immediate start. I put our seven-month-old baby in the bassinet on the back seat (unsecured I might add, as was the way in those days) and drove to the university to let Barrie know. "Hooray," he said to the overseer as he threw his shovel away and got in the car. To me he said, "Goodbye to labouring. For ever". He later told people he'd gone to university but didn't mention that it was to work as a labourer!

Lori with Steven.

Harsant sisters and their children.

CHAPTER 11

Home on the Range

We headed off to Drayton Road, Toowoomba where Barrie rented a duplex for us. We had a bit of furniture, mostly old stuff no longer wanted at the farm, plus a new Pope ringer-model washing machine and electric fridge (what luxury) bought on time payment from an Ipswich store. On the advice from those in-the-know, we took an electric hot-water immerser with us. It proved a most useful accessory as there was no hot water in the duplex laundry.

Toowoomba's tap water was so hard that the soap powder turned to scum as soon as it hit the water, so we had to get a water softener too. In anticipation of the Toowoomba winters, we also took a kerosene heater with us. During Barrie's first week at the new job Steven fell sick and I sat nursing him in front of the heater. There was a doctor's surgery down the road so I took our baby there. Dr Marshall proved wonderful. It turned out that Steven was recovering from a bout of pneumonia while I had a severe case of sinusitis from the dry air caused by the heater. Dr Marshall said I should put a pan of water on top of the heater to get some steam into the air.

It was all part of a steep learning curve in bringing up a baby. Even though I had four younger siblings, I was pretty inexperienced, but I did know about dirty nappies.

Barrie enjoyed realising the dream he'd had while a "dunger" on Culladar and settled into his new job well. Col Joyner was his boss. Some of the other Stock Inspectors were Tom Strachan, Jack Hedges, Bill Cox, Kevin Darcy and Len Penrose. Another inspector, Noel Kalinowski, became a lifelong friend. Noel and his wife, Pat, with their many children, were good company for us and our small child. Indeed there were many good friendships made in Toowoomba.

We never lived near the shops in Toowoomba, so if I wanted to go out to buy the groceries I had to drive Barrie to work then do my shopping and pick him up again in the afternoon, either at the stock office, the Abattoir or the bacon factory where the "stockies" often worked, as they were also qualified Meat Inspectors. By this time we had a Ford Zephyr, but sometimes Barrie had the use of a government ute and could leave me the Zephyr, giving me a bit of freedom.

When the weather warmed up and I took the baby out into the yard, a big drawback of living in Toowoomba became clear. Due to its red soil, the nappies became pinkish red and the "Blue-bag" became a necessity! It was a good place to live in the summer, except for the blowflies. The winters I won't mention, except to say that I owned *three* overcoats.

While stationed in Toowoomba, we became friendly with Stewart and Royal Black who had a farm at Hodgson Vale. We went there on Sunday afternoons to play tennis with many other of their friends. We really enjoyed those afternoons, especially Royal's great sandwiches. It was the first time I had tasted tomato sandwiches with sugar on them. They had two sons, Colin and Bruce, and I believe one stayed on the farm while the other went into television. Since then Toowoomba has spread and their farm is probably now the site of a housing development.

As part of their effort to eradicate Pleuro-Pneumonia in cattle, the Department of Agriculture and Stock chose Barrie to go out west to Boulia. He was issued with a short-wheel-based Willys Jeep, a swag and a two-way radio. It all seemed a great adventure. The radio aerial had a large bullock's shinbone attached to the cord. To get transmission it was hoisted skyward to catch a high tree branch. One of the highlights of the adventure would happen one night when he was camping between Hamilton and Boulia. Min min lights are mysterious glowing lights that bounce along the horizon and Barrie was thrilled to report he'd seen one.

We saw his appointment to Boulia as a good opportunity to save – the additional amount that Barrie would receive for expenses looked like a good lurk. Steven was about 17 months old and I was again pregnant, so we decided to give up our duplex and store the furniture in Toowoomba while I took Steve to live with family in Ipswich, Radford and Southport. (Unfortunately, we would find that the increased cost of living out west ate up most of the expenses!)

After staying for some time at Pommer Street, I shifted from house to house. My stint with the Hunters at Southport suited Steven greatly, there being no kindy in those days. My sister, Barb, and her husband, Bob, had four young children and Steven loved interacting with the other kids. By the time he was two years old, he'd learnt to speak and could recite nursery rhymes. The Hunters were excellent parents and I learnt a lot about bringing up a child while staying with them at Southport.

In the early '60s our friends called our first-born Steven "Little Noosa", referring to our "second honeymoon" spent in that delightful, but now well-known, spot. However, I think the people who so called the baby were about a month off track. Although we did continue to holiday there after our honeymoon. Before we went to Culladar, we had a couple of holidays in "the Woods" at the end of Hastings Street in Noosa, once camping in the back of the Chev. Years later, after we upgraded to a tent, we had 11 inches of rain in one night and were flooded out. Barrie had left Ern and I with baby Steven in a "good" campsite in the 12x12 marquee and he went off to Southport to do some herd recording work. After he left, Ern and I decided that we should put the tent into a superior position and managed to shift camp. Unfortunately we didn't know enough about tents, and left the ropes too tightly pegged down. Consequently, after the heavy rain, the tent leaked and we sat all night watching buckets fill with water leaking from the roof. We weren't too popular when Barrie arrived the next morning, but he soon rectified the errors. Before setting out on that holiday, we had laboriously coated the tent with beeswax and some other product to make it more weatherproof. Barrie always sought good advice before setting out on any new venture.

Barrie spent about five months away on the "Pleuro" altogether. During that time, on July 27, 1961, his dear old Nana, Annie Hughes, died. She had outlasted her husband, William Hughes, by almost 30 years.

I have many fond memories of Nana to this day. She was a stalwart, a great Pommy woman and pioneer. She never completely lost her Pommy accent. In her later years she was a keen television watcher and if a horse and cowboy ran into difficulties in a Western, Nana would exclaim, *Poor bluudy 'orse.* She loved all animals, especially her little dog, Spot, and seemed to feel more compassion for animals than humans. She loved her garden too and had been especially proud of the large collection of hydrangeas that she grew at the front and the side of the house. They often featured in the photos that she sent back to relatives in "The Old Country".

When Barrie returned from Boulia, we moved back to Toowoomba and lived in an old farmhouse in Nelson Street on the south side. In November, a week before our next baby was due, Steven went to his grandparents in Ipswich. As I'd never been parted from him before, I sat around tearfully. We had a monstrous storm that broke windows and piled hail up about a foot deep (30 cm) on the verandas. I bravely hid under the bed.

I had a stew cooking and the hail came in through the window and landed in it! The shock of the storm almost brought on the birth. Luckily I had an appointment with the gynaecologist that afternoon because I was admitted to hospital with hypertension. The next morning I was released and I returned to the farmhouse to await the baby's arrival. Duncan arrived 17 days after Steve's second birthday on November 27, 1961, in the Toowoomba Hospital.

Toowoomba was cold even late in the year and the old house was rickety with plenty of fresh air. To beat the cold, I installed a divan bed for me and two cots for my little sons in the big kitchen. That's where we slept with the old wood stove going all night. After six weeks, Barrie asked plaintively when I'd be returning to the marital bed. "It's so cold on my own," he added. Of course I assented.

Duncan was baptised in St Paul's, Ipswich on April 8, 1962, with Barrie's brother, Don, and my sister, Ann, as godparents.

We moved to a more comfortable house in Alford Street on the northern side of Toowoomba. There we had the luxury of a brick fireplace and a Carmichael stove like the one we had in the cottage on Culladar. To get the best out of the heating facilities, we placed our double bed and two cots in the one bedroom. But there was another reason we all slept in one room – the other bedroom was for motor-mower repairs. Barrie repaired his friends' mowers in his spare time, spreading newspaper over the floor to save the lino from oil and grease. Our one touch of luxury in that house was the black-and-white TV set we rented for a couple of weeks. (We would not *own* a TV until we moved to Noosa in 1980.)

Living in Toowoomba had its funny moments. One day when we were about to head off to Helidon Spa for the Ag. and Stock Christmas break-up picnic, Johnny the sheep dog spotted two Jehovah Witnesses approaching. I'd put the boys in the car and was returning from the kitchen with the very fancy Heavenly Tart I'd made for lunch when Johnny started running up and down inside the fence. Our kelpie was going off his head.

The Jehovah Witnesses asked Barrie a religious question.

"What colour underpants have you got on?" he quipped in reply, meaning: my religion is none of your business. (He could have said "nunya", I suppose.)

They objected to this and began to argue. Barrie had a stockwhip in his hand and started to crack it around their ears (or almost). They decided that discretion was the better part of valour and took off down the street.

In all the hustle and bustle, I dropped the tart on to the rubber floor-mat in the front of the car. I'd spent a lot of time on that blessed tart and was loath to toss it out, so I flipped the floor-mat over and lifted it away from the Heavenly Tart. I tidied my tart up, got rid of the dirty spots and off to the picnic we went. The verdict on my Heavenly Tart was: delicious! On the drive home, I reflected on one of my mother's favourite sayings: *what the eye doesn't see, the heart doesn't grieve.*

The Alford Street house was sold so again we shifted, this time to a house in Volker Street, a country road south of Toowoomba. The immerser was again most valuable in the laundry, but when hanging out nappies the cold winds made my hands bleed. Facilities at the Alford Street house were basic – we had a chip heater in the bathroom and when a billy of milk was required I walked down to the house-owner's dairy. He told me that the paddock over the road where oats grew would be the site of a university for the Darling Downs. Occasionally a snake could be seen coming out of the oat crop to sun itself on the road.

I was pregnant again and one morning, two days before Steven's fourth birthday, I looked out the bedroom window and saw a cow calving. It was an omen, because I soon went into labour. Deborah was born in the Toowoomba Hospital maternity ward on November 9, 1963, some 36 hours after the calf. She was in a posterior position and took her time in arriving. She was my third November baby!

While I was in hospital, Barrie received a transfer. It was to Julia Creek, out West, and we would live in a government-owned residence. I felt apprehensive until the woman sharing my hospital room told me that Julia Creek was a great town. Even though I'd loved the West while we were at Culladar, we were childless then and now we had three littlies to consider. Eventually I became more enthusiastic and began to prepare for the move. I made a mental list: get Deb christened; make new clothes; buy the boys shoes; stock up.

I heard the news of President Kennedy's assassination on the radio, but had little time to think of world events. The departing "Stockie" and his wife kindly sent us a very detailed plan of the house and advised on what would make us comfortable. Buy up before you leave the "Big Smoke", they suggested. I followed their advice – and when the new Myer department store in Toowoomba had a sale, I bought a big roll of lino for the kitchen floor and a new dinner set. (A couple of pieces of that dinner set are still intact in my current kitchen.)

Deb was duly christened on February 8, 1964 in St James Church, Toowoomba by Rev Wicks with our friends, Bill and Norma Cox and Royal Black as her godparents. Bill Cox was a Meat Inspector in the Ag. and Stock Department and a workmate of Barrie's.

Barrie said he wouldn't take the Zephyr to Julia Creek without new tyres and the cost of that was too much. By this time, owing to the Culladar and Boulia jobs, he'd acquired enough "west of the Great Divide" experience to know the importance of good equipment. Barrie was super cautious when tackling anything like a car trip, especially a long one. Everything had to be in A1 condition. So we sold our car.

Before we left for Julia Creek, Barbara and I took our children to Laurel Bank Park for the children to play. All nine of us went in the Hunters' Ford Zephyr. Before I could get baby Deb's bassinet out of the car, the other kids had raced to the slippery slide. In the scramble, Duncan fell from the top of the slide.

Those new shoes! I thought. The soles must be slippery.

It was soon apparent that Duncan was seriously injured so I borrowed the Hunters' car and drove him to our doctor. He didn't stop crying the whole way and was admitted to St Vincent's Hospital in Toowoomba; he'd suffered a fractured skull on the rear left side. It was lucky that Barbara was very good with children, because she had to mind them for hours until I returned to the park.

To make the daily hospital visits we hired a Volkswagen Beetle. We could only take a peep at Duncan for fear the sight of us would excite him too much and interfere with his recovery. On one of our visits a nun commented, "What a fright your boy gave us. He nearly climbed out the window. It's only by the Grace of God that you still have him. He's a real scallywag".

Barrie exploded. "What do you expect with his cot so close to the window! The nurses should be looking after him, not God!"

The poor old nun was shocked but, by our next visit, they'd shifted the cot.

When Duncan came home after a week – the doctor said his skull was stronger than ever – he had acquired a few new habits. Since he had to remain in the cot for another week, he ate his meals there and to our amusement he arranged his place mat, plate and spoon "just so", hospital-style. How very finicky he'd become! I was terrified that he'd fall out of the cot and hurt himself again, and I couldn't eat a bite for days.

Luckily, by the time we headed for The Creek, things were almost back to normal. It was February 1964, and our families were upset at "losing us to the West" again, especially since we now had *three* children. I have to admit that I was getting a little tired of the cleaning involved in leaving yet another abode. (Little did I realise that the move to Julia Creek was just the start of it. By the time we retired to Karrabin, where I now live, we'd moved 15 times!) My motto was: *I work better under pressure.* When my spirits flagged and I wondered "Why me?" my motto spurred me on.

Our goods and chattels preceded us and we had free rail travel to Julia Creek, with sleepers for the five of us. After the comfort of the *Sunlander*'s air-conditioned carriages, it was a shock to step into the steam bath of Townsville. It was hot yet barely 6am. Welcome to the tropics! We spent the day in Townsville and caught the *Inlander* that evening. After hours on the train, we pulled into the Julia Creek Railway Station to begin a new Western adventure, this time with three young children in tow. Johnny the dog stayed behind with the Patricks.

Barrie goes to Boulia.

'Hit the Road Jack' — Steven says goodbye to Barrie as he heads west.

A Harsant family gathering.

Lori on Cobra.

QT Xmas party dress-ups.

Harsant girls with their parents and beaux.

Fishing at Culladar.

Eva Patrick's violin graduation.

Ern Patrick.

Blue Heeler Hotel, Kynuna.

Deb's Christening.

Barrie with Beth Garrett on This is Your Life.

A return trip to the Blue Heeler with sister, Barbara.

Visiting the Crewe house.

Grandchildren, Harry and Bronte.

CHAPTER 12

Faraway Places

Although different from the dry plains of Winton, the Julia Creek insects soon had us reverting to the old "Queensland salute". There'd been a good Wet and all the insects imaginable – flies, sandflies, gidgee bugs, beetles and mosquitoes – made us welcome. Typical of February in the north-west.

Our furniture and effects had already arrived at Julia Creek, affectionately known to locals as The Creek. Joe Lucas, the local carrier, had collected them from the railway station and moved them into our residence. (In later years, Joe became a very close and valued friend and employee.) We inspected the house and I was impressed by its size and the fact its 35 sets of casement windows had flyscreens. Our boxes still needed to be unpacked so Barrie took us to Gannon's Hotel, where we were due to spend the night, while he acquainted himself with his new domain, not only his office, but the police station, school, doctor, hospital and bakery.

Gannon's was most uncomfortable for someone straight out of Toowoomba with three littlies. Our beds (with obligatory mosquito nets) were on a veranda with bare, splintery floorboards under an unlined, hot tin roof. It was so hot I was flat out keeping baby Deb from dehydrating. The toilet –

the type emptied once a week by the sanitary man – was in the back yard. Of course Steven and Duncan wanted to keep "going". When Barrie returned in possession of his work vehicle, a Holden ute circa 1963, I told him I'd rather sleep on the floor in the government residence than here in the hotel, so off we went.

We filled our brand-new Bon-Air portable air-conditioner with water and put it in front of Deb's cot. The rest of us slept on mattresses on the floor with every window and floor-level louvre open. Welcome to Julia Creek! Our first night gave little hint of the very enjoyable and highly social couple of years we would spend in The Creek. Although we never did get used to the heat!

We soon unpacked our goods and chattels and settled into our new home. The new lino was nice, but the back-yard dunny wasn't. It was a fair distance from the house, which meant escorting the kids there and back through the long grass when they wanted to "go" to guard them against snakes. Snakes were plentiful, front and back. Once I was breastfeeding Deb on the veranda when one of the workmen doing up the road in front of the house called out, "There's a big brown in your yard, missus". I put the baby down, grabbed a nearby hoe and cut the old "Joe Blake" in half. The boys played in that yard!

The town water, artesian or sub-artesian, was undrinkable and had the rotten-egg smell common out West, an aroma that soon became familiar. The water did, however, make for good dental health if you dared – few people who drank it ever needed the dentist, although it did leave white stains on the teeth of the young. Despite the fact it didn't rain all that often, we had a couple of rainwater tanks and I gave the kids fluoride tablets daily. Sewerage came to us during our tenancy, involving another renovated bathroom and a toilet in the house – a great improvement. Out West, the Queensland Government charged low rents for their houses, but the cost of living was high. A cabbage in Sills' fruit shop, a very wilted object, cost three times that of a fresh one in Toowoomba.

Our next-door neighbour was a poor manager. It was nothing for one of the children to come in and say, "Could Mum borrow some washing powder? She wants to do some washing". The best one was whether she could borrow a cup of rice and a bit of curry powder, as she wanted to make curry and rice for tea. She had a lovely new car that I envied, but the poor woman was "sick" every Child Endowment day (the forerunner of the current Social Security benefits to assist parents) so needed to go up the street for "medicine". It must have been pretty potent stuff because she once hit the gatepost driving in the yard on her return home! One day she threw all the kids, clothes, tennis racquets and toys into the car and took off. The clothes on the line hung there for weeks. I think her poor old hubby didn't have the heart to take them off, although he must have enjoyed the peace and not having things thrown at him regularly, like crockery for instance. She was never our neighbour again.

Duncan had an ear infection once, but our main health problem was Sandy Blight, a very uncomfortable eye problem that was rampant among children in the outback. The kids often wore fly veils on their hats to prevent fly bites and gradually gained immunity to the Blight. On one occasion, Deb became ill with an upper respiratory tract infection and Dr Tony admitted her to the Julia Creek Hospital. After settling the boys down for the night, I visited her. There she was in only a singlet and nappy on the hospital veranda fanned by a cold, wet wind. I blew up and the person in charge was sacked on the spot. Our doctor stayed at the hospital all night to watch her. Deb spent a few more days in hospital with a case of pneumonia.

Despite such instances, the West was generally a pretty healthy place to bring up a family.

Steven started school the following year. One day shortly after starting school he told me he'd found a £1 note on the footpath near the school. "Where's it now?" I asked. "Oh," he said, "a couple of big boys came along and said they'd just lost it. They told me that I should give it to them, which I did." He had a lot to learn about human nature.

The boys competed in the swimming carnivals and Steven won a couple of races, the son of the ambulance man his main competition. At only three Duncan could swim across the pool, and by the time we left The Creek, Deb was learning to swim at two years of age. (She would become a very good swimmer making me think: maybe it's in the blood. According to a certificate and medal from the Qld Amateur Swimming Society dated March 20, 1926, Ern Patrick swam three miles in 108 mins 2 seconds. I think that might have been in the Bremer River. Barrie was also a good swimmer and won trophies at the IGS for swimming.) Perhaps Deb's love of swimming started in Julia Creek.

The West is certainly a land of contrasts. It wasn't unusual to have temperatures below freezing in the winter and up to 45C degrees in the summer. It was great to have the town pool in those high temperatures. It was even more fortunate that the swimming pool was right across the road from our house.

As we had no car, I did a lot of walking with Deb on board our little stroller, and sometimes Duncan if his young legs tired. There were no concrete paths in our street so the going was rough, but it was good exercise. Luckily we were pretty close to the school, the shops, the post office and the bank. The baker was further away, but I only had to push the stroller there on the days Barrie was out bush, because when in town and working in the office he brought home a fresh loaf of delicious bread for lunch.

I wanted to make some extra money and started dressmaking. As well as making to order for a couple of ladies, I replaced zips, repaired trousers and shirts, let out and took in seams and turned shirt collars (a popular way to get a few more months out of a collared shirt). I also made children's clothes, often copying the styles from the displays in the window of the local dress shop. I made all our kids' clothes, except their hats and socks. Ern's old singlets, for example, made good children's singlets. While I sewed, the children played on the big veranda that surrounded the house on three sides. We had bought a trike and a pedal car and they rode them around and around. I took my garments to Mrs Hayhoe, the hairdresser, to sell. Her salon was on her front veranda. I also made board shorts for her many boys. Mrs Hayhoe was a pianist in a dance band with her husband and I sometimes played extras for them on the piano while they took a break (and maybe a sneaky drink out the back). On occasion, I joined in on my piano-accordion.

A major source of entertainment at The Creek was the arrival of a Fokker Friendship on Sunday afternoons. It was an opportunity for "a sticky-beak" at who was arriving in town by air and we joined other townfolk in visiting the airstrip to watch it land. Before the Fokker's ETA, someone would ensure that the landing strip was free of stock or kangaroos. After the newsagent, or his emissary, collected his bundles of the *Sunday Mail* and *Truth* newspapers the plane took off for The Curry and The Isa (Cloncurry and Mount Isa). Everyone then returned to the newsagency in town to queue up and buy their Sunday papers.

For the first time since our marriage we had a phone in the house. If the office was unattended, graziers and drovers phoned our residence. Barrie often had out-of-town jobs where he'd visit stations, work with graziers, and check the permits of the drovers on the road with their stock. Tick control was a priority. Barrie used his bare fingernails (called "scratching for ticks") on stock travelling from one place to another. The smallest tick found on one beast could mean the whole herd, usually many hundreds, had to be dipped before proceeding on their way. Barrie would then supervise the dipping of the cattle. On his return I would hand him a heap of messages. Without clerical assistance in many government-run offices, the Government had free secretarial help from the wives. I suppose the managers of the Public Service considered our services a fair exchange for the slightly cheaper rent on a government residence, but I think the Stock Inspector's wife should be paid something for her contribution to the economy.

A lot of stock activity occurred at Sedan Dip, north of Julia Creek, where travelling cattle were dipped. Barrie made a lot of good friends among the drovers, including Tiddley Triffett.

During our stay in Julia Creek, Barrie did another stint in
Boulia for the Pleuro Campaign and another Stock Inspector
was based in Julia Creek to do the normal day-to-day running
of the stock district in his absence. Some of the graziers in
the Channel Country used "Bronco Branding" on their stock,
which interested Barrie. It involved pulling a beast up to a yard
fence with a rope by a man on horseback to brand the young
animal. Barrie referred to that procedure when people wondered
about the name of the Broncos, his beloved football team, when
"bronco" was supposedly an Americanism. It was definitely
an outback and commonly used procedure and expression.
An outback town, Stonehenge I think, now has an annual
competition in the art.

The Stock Inspector (dubbed a Stockie) often did veterinary
work, as the nearest vet was at the Toorak Research Station,
some 25 miles south of The Creek. The Presbyterian Minister
who lived opposite our house had a cat. Some hoodlums had
tried to castrate poor old "pussy" with what could have been
a jam-tin lid, so jagged were the cuts. The cat required quite a
few stitches, courtesy of Barrie.

Luckily, The Creek had very few hoodlums. That had a lot
to do with the good police staff, but the drinking age limit of
21 was a good steadier and young people were different in the
'60s with few able to afford a car. Sergeant Gabriel, the officer-
in-charge, had his constable drive him slowly around the town
every evening just before sunset – this helped too.

Here we were in the land of the Akubra, Stetson, R.M.
Williams, kite hawks, galahs, dust and roly-poly, the plant that
blows in the desert winds. Similar geography, but a long way
from the Dunger Days on Culladar. Here in Julia Creek our
friends included drovers, public servants, business professionals,
graziers, stock and station agents, the chemist, the doctor
and the vet. No class distinction here. And we were veritable
social butterflies! The social scene was hectic, especially around
Christmas. One year we were out 12 nights out of 14. The
Common Ranger's daughter in the street behind us obliged by

babysitting if it was an adult-only occasion such as a ball. The Civic Centre, the hub of all big events, was only a short way down the street, as were most places of interest in The Creek.

We attended dances, pictures and the Annual Dinner of the Masonic Lodge, of which Barrie was a member, and visited the homes of friends. Barrie played golf and became C Grade champion a couple of times, taking out the title on sand greens. There were many golf-club parties to go to. With three young children to take care of, it never occurred to me to play golf, but some of the women did.

The Julia Creek sports days, held on the football field across the road from our house, were more my scene and I entered in various events on such occasions as well as the ladies' races at district events. When I was about 30 I won the female 100-yard sprint against younger ladies. Barrie was very proud of me, especially when we heard that the Shire Chairman had a few bob on one of my opponents known to have a fair turn of pace. The sports days went on into the night with a mardi gras. Barrie helped on the hamburger stall for a while one year with Father Garvey and Jumbo Harris. People are different out West, even priests. As he cooked on the barbecue on a truck trailer, Father Garvey sang: *Who called the cook a bastard? Who called the bastard a cook?* I remember a sports night with a freezing temperature and mugs of wonderful homemade soups, antidotes against turning into an ice-block.

Horseracing in the bush was also big on the social calendar. Race days were fashion parades, so the ladies-wear shops did a good trade in frocks and hats. The kids and I only went to Julia Creek and Sedan Dip meetings, but Barrie, as part of his duties, went to Cloncurry, Kynuna, McKinlay, Richmond and other small meetings. He was on duty to issue and check permits, scratch for ticks and to spray horses. As we didn't have a private vehicle, the three kids and I went along with Barrie in the government Holden ute. There were no seatbelts or rules on passenger numbers in the early '60s so the five of us squashed into the front seat but that didn't matter. The children were always very well-behaved and we often sat around after the races, waiting until Barrie finished his work. A ride in the ute occasionally was fair exchange for my unpaid secretarial duties as a Stockie's wife, I thought.

One day I was sitting in the Holden, waiting for Barrie to knock off, when I saw a drunk lying under a nearby vehicle. The unfortunate man was run over, twice, by the vehicle owner. He looked very green by the time the driver realised his mistake.

Sergeant Gabriel had a unique way of settling trouble if anyone got "fighting drunk" at the races. He put the troublemakers in a ring and let them fight it out. They were usually too drunk to get in many hits, but it satisfied their desire for a fight. Balls or dances followed the races, going until sun-up, when breakfast was served.

The newsagent's wife organised the Debutante Balls at the Civic Centre. One year she asked me to play the piano for the Debs and their partners and promised me a nice piece of Wedgwood pottery from their shop as payment. (In the end she forgot!) The night of that ball became a nightmare for me. I was wearing a lovely homemade two-piece evening gown. While getting into the car, I brushed up against the door catch, and my lined mauve number came into contact with grease on the fitting. I raced back inside to clean it up and in my rush saturated the spot with dry-cleaning fluid. It soaked right through the material into my skin. I had a painful right hip for the rest of the night and some big blisters for days. A salutary lesson on how *not* to use dry-cleaning fluid! (Luckily, it did remove the grease.)

One morning after a late night at a ball, some friendly fire brigade members led by Jumbo Harris invaded our house. They woke us, made us a cup of tea and got us out of bed. "We're having a special brigade practice," they explained. The usual fire practice siren went off at 7.30pm every Wednesday.

I only remember a couple of fires during our stay in Julia Creek. Once when a house burnt down a couple of doors up from us, Barrie very heroically raced in and rescued a couple of gas cylinders. The other fire I recall was when a drover was smoking in a toilet where saddles were stored. Somehow a saddle caught fire. Fortunately that place was not far from the fire station and was saved.

Littlies in Julia Creek.

Barrie near Bedourie.

CHAPTER 13

Kegs, Kids and Cattle Dogs

After 18 months in Julia Creek, Les Llewellyn, a publican friend of Barrie, told him that the run-down Kynuna Hotel, 75 miles south of The Creek on the Landsborough Highway, was for sale. "Buy it, Barrie," he urged. "Turn it into a goer." Of course this appealed to Barrie. Although he was a very cautious person by nature, he insisted that we go and inspect it. My plea that I'd be no good in a hotel, especially with three "billy lids" to take care of, didn't divert him at all.

I'd heard about the "Kynuna Ladies", a mob of goats that inhabited the township and apparently stood on cars in their efforts to reach foliage on trees, but that was all I knew about Kynuna. I had mixed feelings. The thought of getting stuck into and creating something out of the old joint had a certain attraction, having tarted up so many old rental houses throughout my married life. I agreed "to look", thinking: we have no money to do it anyway! Who would lend us the required deposit and why leave the comfortable and pleasant life with a steady pay cheque we led in Julia Creek? I also gave thought to the years of study and hopes to achieve this government position and felt, like others, that it would be a big sacrifice to give it up. It was difficult as a wage earner, however, to acquire assets for the future and owning a business, especially as there was no capital gains tax, suggested a way to rectify this.

On our visit I don't recall seeing any goats, but I remember the kite hawks, willy-willies and tumbleweeds that greeted us. The township was experiencing a bad drought that year and it appeared to be one big vista of gibber-stones, with a shop, post office, CWA hall, small school and a few old houses sitting on a dry, stony ridge.

And of course, an old pub.

While inspecting the hotel, we saw a storm building up in the north towards Julia Creek, but thought we'd miss it. However, halfway through the late-afternoon journey home, the rain came down and we became hopelessly bogged. What a time for the drought to break! We appeared to be the only silly buggers on the road so there was nothing we could do but to settle down for the night. Barrie sheltered under the tonneau cover in the back of the ute in his swag and I settled down in the front with the children. I put Deb on the parcel rack behind the seat, Steven on the seat and Duncan on the floor at my feet. What a night! Duncan had a high temperature and vomited all night. Rain or not, I had to keep opening the door to facilitate the action – at least the rain helped wash it away! I was very worried about him.

The next morning we were glad to see Joe Lucas's mail truck approaching at full bore down the road on its way to Kynuna. One of Joe's boys was driving, but I can't remember which lad it was, Robert, Noel or Vince. As he neared us, his truck went into a big skid. He managed to avoid hitting us and gave us a wide grin as his truck came to a stop. He pulled us out of the bog and we continued on. The storm must have been a narrow one, because we had no trouble getting back to The Creek.

Duncan was still sick so I asked the doctor to call. After taking a look at him the doctor diagnosed a bad ear infection. We asked Duncan why he hadn't told us his ear was sore. "When Dad had a sore ear," he said, "he had to have a needle, and I don't like needles." Duncan had an aversion to medicines of all sorts. Although he was four years and nine months at the time, he preferred to put up with the pain. It took two of us holding him down to get him to take a dose of what the doctor prescribed.

One of my worries about going to Kynuna to live was the distance from medical help. Barrie allayed my fears by reminding me that the Royal Flying Doctor Service (RFDS) was always on hand.

Our brother-in-law, Bob Hunter, wrote to us and stressed the advantages of being in business – remember that superannuation was not great in those days – as well as offering us his and Barb's best wishes. Barrie decided to go to Townsville to ask Burns, Philp and Company Ltd (Burns Philp) to finance us to buy the pub.

When he went to buy his plane ticket the agent said, "You're brave. The plane to Mount Isa crashed near Winton only a couple of hours ago".

"Couldn't happen again so soon," Barrie responded, and bought a seat on the next day's flight. It was an Ansett/ANA Viscount that went down on September 22, 1966, 13.5 miles west of Winton. All 20 passengers and four crew were killed.

Barrie's visit to Burns Philp was successful. The firm was very trusting of us, for we had no experience. They must have been impressed by our good references because they lent us the whole amount, $14,000 at 10% interest over 10 years I think it was. We then negotiated with Jack Cramp, the pub's owner, and Barrie applied for a Liquor Licence from the Licensing Commission in Brisbane, which was granted immediately.

With Barrie's super and holiday pay we bought an old Chev truck and enough stock to get started. (We bought the truck intending to do our own carrying, but the pub would become so busy that it wasn't viable to have one of us away regularly. As it turned out, we would have been better off with a normal car.) Burns Philp gave us our liquor, cigarettes and other stock on credit, and other suppliers did the same for soft drinks, bakery items, meat and groceries. We were in business!

We sent our furniture ahead with Joe Lucas – his stock truck had more than one purpose! We headed for Kynuna with kegs, dogs, groceries, soft drinks, brooms, buckets and mops on the back of the Chev and the five of us once again in the cab of the vehicle. The last things packed were, as always, the mop and broom. Another residence left clean and neat!

Imagine the sight of us rolling into Kynuna in the old Chev with the dogs standing on the beer kegs! The whole town turned out to see the sight. What a hoo-ha.

The following is a description of Kynuna, our new bailiwick. It was compiled by one of the teachers with the help of the school kids, and I found it in a school magazine:

Kynuna has a population of 35, and is situated 110 miles-north west of Winton, 114 miles south-east of Cloncurry, and 75 miles south of Julia Creek. It is slightly south of the Dividing Range, being the watershed between the Gulf Rivers to the North and the Lake Eyre catchment rivers to the south. Kynuna's average rainfall is 15 inches, and the district produces wool and beef.

Kynuna township consists of a post office, police station, school, hotel, general store, CWA hall and seven houses. The township is situated on the Landsborough Highway between Winton and Mount Isa. There is no electricity supply in Kynuna, and most houses have their own generating plant for lights. The water supply comes from an artesian bore, which is approximately 3000 feet deep. Today this water is 300 feet from the surface, and is brought up with the aid of a windmill. The water is pumped into overhead tanks for storage, and also to allow the water to cool, as artesian water is very hot. The water has a high mineral content and is thus not suitable for lawns and gardens. The largest property in the district is Kynuna Station with an area of 230,000 acres. The Kynuna district is at the headwaters of the Diamantina River, which flows into Lake Eyre in South Australia.

The Diamantina River at Kynuna can spread to three miles wide during the wet season, but the river is dry for nine months of the year. The Combo Waterhole, famous for the poem "Waltzing Matilda", is part of the Diamantina River, 12 miles from Kynuna. Kynuna is on the stock route for animals travelling south on foot from the Northern Territory and the Gulf Country. These days much of the stock is transported by road-train, some trucks taking as many as 60 head of stock at a time.

Barrie told Jack Cramp he wanted all staff gone by morning because we couldn't afford to pay anyone. Jean Jackson, a local character known for always wearing an apron, was helping behind the bar at the time. I had practically no knowledge of hotels so had a lot to learn. I received a few lessons at pulling beer on the first night and of necessity it had to be a quick lesson. You learn fast when you must. At closing time after Jack's farewell, we paid him for all the change he had left in the till, an old wooden drawer under the bar. Jack took off in his old truck the next morning and left us to our own devices. It was rumoured that he had wads of money in the drain pipes at the Julia Creek racecourse and in milk tins around and under the pub. It was also rumoured that he ran a "book" on the side. We found plenty of old tins and bottles in the yard, but no money.

The morning of October 26, 1966 was the start of a stretch of hard labour, fun, lots of joy and much adversity. Working at least 16 hours a day, seven days a week is quite a call on a person's stamina but, with a few exceptions, we did it for nearly 14 years. Making a profit and paying off debt was a strong incentive to keep going, and the longer you slaved the more used to it you became.

On our first morning we did a stocktake. It didn't take long. We had to stock up from scratch, in a small way at first. There was no food in the pub except for a string of old sausages hanging in the cold room that even the dogs wouldn't eat. Our suppliers would prove very trusting, but we had a good name and they were glad of a new, reliable customer. After we became established we would order most things in bulk, including tins of ham, bags of sugar, drums of flour and powdered milk. We used old milk and cream cans from the Radford dairy for storage. We continued to patronise the baker in Julia Creek. He must have been pleased to see our daily order of a loaf of bread rocket! Owing to the vagaries of the weather, it pays to be well-stocked in the bush. Kynuna's local store had the odd necessity, but not in the proportions we needed. People said a former shopkeeper, Tom Pattel, sold everything from a needle to an anchor. Someone tested the anchor assertion once and Tommy pulled one from under the counter. He had ordered it for a customer preparing for a Diamantina flood, but they never collected it.

Eight months before we became publicans (on February 14, 1966), Australia converted to decimal currency. On that day, I went to the bank in Julia Creek to withdraw money and then to the grocery shop where I was served by the elderly owner. She didn't miss a beat, taking to decimal currency straight away. So when we started in the pub I thought, if Mrs Coleman can do it, so can I. Handling all the money quickly *was* a new experience. We didn't have a mechanised till in the pub, so adding up in our heads was necessary. Fortunately our education gave us a good grounding and it soon became second nature, although Barrie took a long time to stop referring to pounds, shillings and pence.

It became obvious on the very first day that the cold room was deficient and urgent action was needed or we'd lose our perishables. Aside from that, keg beer hadn't been sold in Kynuna for many years and having it icy cold was a must. Keith Coleman, a good refrigeration mechanic from Julia Creek, came to the rescue. He put gas in the system and got the cold room working well. It must have been a long time since anyone had a cold drink at the Kynuna Hotel.

A galvanised iron watertank in the cold room with a tap delivered cold water to the bar. A hose from a tap in the yard filled the tank. After the brine tanks, the method of cooling, started to work, everything froze. When the water eventually started to come out it was in the form of ropey strings of green slime. It hadn't been cleaned for decades! We wondered about the state of the water that travellers and locals had been drinking so innocently. We disconnected the tank and scrubbed it out. It's a wonder it hadn't killed someone.

There was no treatment plant for the town water, which was a direct-feed from the mill tank to the houses in town. It was very good water, but left a white stain on the kids' teeth as in Julia Creek. Some of the young people who lived in Kynuna all their lives were able to boast of never needing the services of a dentist, some of them in their 20s. Maybe their sensible plain bush diet also contributed. We all drank the town water, and I no longer gave the children fluoride tablets.

Once when the council workers came to do some maintenance on the windmill they took great delight in telling us about all the dead galahs, rubbish and bird poo they cleaned out of the uncovered tank. On a still day there was a diesel motor for stand-by power, maintained by one of the men in town.

Two Southern Cross diesel motors, in an old corrugated iron shed in the back yard, supplied power to the hotel. One engine powered the cold room and the other one the lighting. Sixteen two-volt batteries were connected to the lighting engine for storage, thence to the 32-volt lights and appliances such as the fan, a Bon Air and our washing machine. A fan was essential in the cold room to move the air chilled by the brine tanks. The engines would prove to be the bane of our lives until mains power was connected from Julia Creek, 13 years later! If a motor broke down, it would invariably be at the most inconvenient time – during the Wet or when there was a big crowd expected. Getting engine parts in a wet season often involved having them dropped from a light aircraft in corn bags, and hopefully, if the man flying the plane was accurate, into the prickly bush gully across the road from the pub. We often had food dropped by the same method. No eggs naturally!

Bill Trifett was the first motor mechanic we used and later Bobby Rose. Both were excellent, and when Joe Lucas came to help out he gave us wonderful support with his knowledge of anything mechanical. If the lighting plant broke down we would resort to carbide, gas or kerosene lights and candles. We had no answer for a broken-down cold-room motor though.

One part of my education in running the pub was learning how to fuel up and start the old diesels. It was quite a heavy job, with the big fly-wheel, but my experience of diesel motors in the dairy partially prepared me. Battery levels were regularly checked with a hydrometer.

We had a big opening night. We were gratified by the support from the locals and passing traffic and seeing some cash coming in. We met many people that night who would ultimately become lifelong friends. Our truckie customers immediately started to spread the word, "You can get a cold beer and a good feed at Kynuna at last".

On the October morning after take-over in 1966, I entered the kitchen and it was clear I had a lot of work ahead of me. Jack Cramp had used the wood fire daily to make his cuppa, even though there was a gas stove. The ceilings and walls of that kitchen would take me and Netta, a lady from nearby Mimong Station, days to clean. They were "smoked" for years. The ceiling looked like a draughtboard where some squares were cleaned and others weren't. (We'd eventually have two gas stoves, side by side, and many years later a microwave oven. Goodbye wood stove!)

We needed plenty of energy to make things liveable and clean initially. I don't think the Licensing Commission inspectors had paid too many visits before we took over.

Perhaps the turnover was so small they didn't think it worth the trouble.

We had an old fellow known as Mad Mick down from Julia Creek to help in the clean-up around and under the buildings. As these were only about 45cm off the ground, it was a difficult job. The Sergeant of Police in Julia Creek had asked us to take Mick with us, to keep him off the grog for a while and to give The Creek locals a bit of a break. I can't remember his surname, but he was Irish and his first name was Mick, "for shure".

Mad Mick apparently had some pub or catering experience, because when he saw me making sandwiches he said, "After you spread the butter on, Missus, scrape it off because it'll go twice as far, for shure". (Actually, we bought margarine by the carton because of its spreadability and kept it in the cold room. We had butter on the dining tables though, often sitting in nests of ice to prevent melting in our non air-conditioned dining room.)

In that first week when Mad Mick cleaned up the 50 years' worth of cans and bottles from around the premises, the interiors had to be done from top to bottom. Besides the main building of the pub, the premises consisted of a separate building of six twin bedrooms.

The beds were old black iron bedsteads that I heard came from the Kynuna Hospital when it closed, circa 1939-40. Kynuna shrank after the Townsville-Mount Isa Railway line came into existence. (The school, I believe, also used buildings from that old hospital.) In the old days, Kynuna had more than one pub.

We put some new lino down in the rooms and cleaned the walls and windows. We replaced the old horsehair mattresses, bought new linen, towels and bedspreads and, although not salubrious, knew they would suffice to give many a traveller a good night's rest for years to come.

The Ladies and Gents toilets and bathrooms were on the far end of the bedrooms. Just past the toilets was the "donkey", a hot-water system. It comprised of a heavy 44-gallon drum with fittings attached, heated by a wood fire, and piped to the bathrooms. It was a very effective hot-water system, and during races or rodeos when there was an influx of guests as well as the normal travelling public, it was kept stoked night and day – usually by men on their way to the Gents. Competitors at these events made use of our bathing facilities. If there was a rodeo coming up at Kynuna, Cloncurry or Mount Isa, a lot of the competitors camped at the pub for a few days to rest their horses and themselves. Many truckies, on pulling up, headed straight for the pub's shower with towel and toiletries under an arm. They liked to clean up before coming into the bar for a drink and a meal.

The septic system would cause us a lot of headaches, particularly when an unthinking traveller put a comic book or another unmentionable down the loo. When the tank was pumped out it would produce everything including condoms, bras, undies, swimmers and books. We once had it emptied by a man who was working on the main road putting in culverts with his cement-mixing truck. His name was Sofranoff and he was amazed at what came out of that tank. He also cemented the back yard for us, which we turned into a sort of a beer garden. The concrete mixer had more than one use.

The main building of the pub consisted of living quarters that we occupied, an office, bar, cold room, storage space, lounge, dining room and kitchen.

One day a couple of months after we took over, Mad Mick pointed to the dirt area on the eastern side and said, "You'll have lawn on that piece of land in the morning!" We laughed, but Mick got an early start the next day and transplanted couch grass from a ditch down the back where the waste water went. So began our lawn, which would thrive on the local bore water.

Mick, who was able to pick up a brolga and nurse it, would eventually leave our employ. Barrie "rationed" him to a couple of stubbies a night, but it wasn't enough and when he could no longer go without a "skinful" we were left without a yardman and another set of hands to help when the tourist coaches arrived.

The lawn became a popular place. Many a truckie rested there in the shade of the pub on a hot afternoon. Barrie and I would be lucky if we managed to rest there *at all*. One regular truckie had an artificial leg and he often lay down on the grass for a kip, his leg placed near his arms. Our kids were most intrigued. He'd get a laugh out of it and played it up to them.

The pub lawn was the only patch of green grass for miles. The kids liked to play there. Steven, now seven, wrote to his grandparents about the novelty of it. He mentioned that he, Duncan and Kevin Begg, the storekeeper's son, played football on the lawn. One night, Barrie and Ron Teece, whose two boys were about the same age as our lads, set up a boxing match for the boys using Barrie's full-size boxing gloves. One bout was under way between the five-year-old boys when Duncan stopped and scratched around on the ground while still wearing his boxing gloves.

"What's the matter?" he was asked.

"Young Teecie knocked out one of my teeth. I've gotta find it otherwise I won't get any money from the Tooth Fairy."

On the other side of the lawn was an old storage building where the yardman, when we had one, camped, with the laundry on one end. Some people called it the Drunks' Quarters. In previous years, drunks were sent there to sober-up.

The cold room held our most perishable goods until a truckie friend, Alan Girdler, made us a 240-volt motor-driven box freezer. We bought a motor to run it. Alan transported frozen foods and he delivered frozen chooks and other cold goods to us from Provincial Traders, a wholesaler in Mount Isa. If he wasn't out our way for some time we had shippers, with dry ice, railed to Julia Creek to meet the mail truck, always hoping there were no hold-ups and that the frozen goods arrived in as good a condition as when they left The Isa.

After establishing ourselves as a customer with the firm, we did a steady business of cooked chooks over the counter. This was a new innovation for Kynuna, as were the hot dogs, hamburgers, sandwiches, hot pies and small cold meat sausages like Ham Delight or Strasbourg. All made easier by the introduction of the freezer to complement the cold room and keep the bread fresh. The freezer also allowed us to keep a much bigger stock of fresh meat, enabling us to feed a fairly large clientele if ever we had a Wet and consequently a crowd stuck in town, or a sudden order for meals from an approaching coachload of tourists. When we bought a side of beef we'd hope with fingers crossed that our freezer kept working.

Three mail trucks visited Kynuna weekly. The Julia Creek and Winton runs delivered goods from either town's rail service, whichever suited at the time. The McKinlay weekly mail could not offer us that facility as it was not on the railway line. Large quantities of tinned food, including beetroot, peas, beans and pineapple, were always in our larder to meet all contingencies – you never know in the bush. We also bought our fruit and vegies by the carton. For many years we lived on mutton, which we were used to after being on Culladar, and it kept well hanging in the cold room. We obtained this commodity locally. Very good it was, too.

The big freezer was also very useful in another way. We made and sold ice that we set in various containers, including jam and fruit tins. We had a special canvas bag to crush the ice into smaller pieces with the aid of a hammer. Ice had never been sold in Kynuna before and it was much appreciated by the travelling public.

One of the delicacies enjoyed by the truckies and others was yellow-belly caught in the Combo Waterhole. After a few days hanging in the cold room it was really delicious. They are an oily fish and hanging dried them out a little. We had no time to go fishing, but at times locals and friends from Julia Creek gave us some of their catch. Some truckies always asked if yellow-belly was on the menu.

We were inundated once with banana prawns from the Gulf when a fridge van on its way to Brisbane rolled on the Julia Creek road. I cooked many big meat-boilers full of the much desired and rare delicacy, which were enjoyed by anyone who called in. Travellers boiled them up over camp-fires too, and truckies cooked them for days and the whole place had a very strong smell of old prawn shells.

During our first year at the pub, a local brought in a plain turkey (or bustard) to cook for a birthday dinner for me. I wasn't aware at that stage that killing turkeys was against the law and possibly the one we cooked was not deliberately shot but hit by a car and retrieved while still fresh. I think it was a bit of an April Fools' trick, as the turkey meat did not please the taste buds at all. However, if you were caught out bush and near to starving, I guess the plain turkey would be delicious.

Our rubbish dump was a prickly bush gully about 100 yards from the back of the pub. Prickly bushes such as mimosa and parkinsonia were about the only things to grow naturally. The kids had a whale of a time in a dump near the gully uncovering old bottles from a previous century. We ended up with quite a collection, including purple castor-oil bottles, those with marble stoppers and bottles that couldn't stand up for their rounded bases. I wonder now how the antique bottles survived previous floods.

When they became old enough to back a trailer with the car, at about eight years of age, the boys emptied our bottles and cans and other bar rubbish into the gully.

After a big flood, the rubbish probably stretched from our pub to Lake Eyre. So, after a couple of floods we decided that the dump wasn't well placed and we used a dump out of town with the help of Joe Lucas, who allowed the kids to drive his vehicle, off-road of course. Deb helped too. (When the boys both left Kynuna for high school in Ipswich years later, she took over the job, solo.)

After two months of cleaning, we prepared for our first pub Christmas. The usual Kynuna tradition was a Christmas tree party held in the CWA Hall for the youngsters of the district, with Stumpy Malone one year transporting "Santa" in his sulky, drawn by a lovely white pony. The nights usually ended up being a celebration that continued in the pub. When we arrived at Kynuna, half the district (or so it seemed) wanted the novelty of Christmas dinner in the pub.

At the Christmas Eve party we told revellers to stock up on beer, cigarettes and their Bex or Vincent's APCs before they went home because we wanted a sleep-in on the 25th, one of the only two days off a year we had. This passed over their heads because some locals woke us up early wanting cigarettes and soft drinks, and naturally the kids were anxious to open presents once they'd woken. So much for a sleep-in.

After the presents were opened and we had phoned our parents, I attacked the kitchen. We invited any local ringers and truckies, who would have otherwise spent a lonely Christmas Day, to join us for lunch. My challenge was to single-handedly "produce". Frankly, it was an absolute nightmare. Apart from stirring the Christmas pud for luck, the kids were too small to help. No help from Barrie either, as the "illegals" in the bar kept him busy. We had no staff at this stage and licensing laws did not allow the pub to be open on Christmas Day, except for guests in the hotel rooms. Needless to say we had a register full of names. The policeman must have been away.

The customers were happy to keep drinking and didn't seem perturbed when Christmas lunch was finally served at 3pm. The food was OK but the cook was jiggered by the end of the day. It was one of the most stressful days of my life. The heat of course was awful, because we had to have all the doors closed according to the licensing laws and the poor old 32-volt Bon Air and a little fan were small consolations. The temperature in the kitchen was about 48 degrees Celsius (115-120 Fahrenheit), normal for a summer day in Kynuna.

The stress of the day was broken by a chap from Julia Creek who told us about his Christmas Eve the year before.

He got up during the hot December night, he said, to the call of nature. "Gee it's cold out there," he said to his wife when he went back to bed. "I opened the toilet door and it was freezing."

"Be quiet and go back to sleep," his missus ordered, "you're drunk."

Next morning when she went to the fridge to prepare for Christmas lunch, she realised her old man had mistaken the fridge for the loo.

"You dirty bastard," she said. "You've ruined the ham and the trifle."

Kids and the old Chev.

Stirring the Christmas pud.

CHAPTER 14

Ever the Showman

When we entered the hotel business Barrie said he would start as he meant to continue: be tough right from the start; let people know how we intended to run the business; no fighting; no swearing and no causing trouble. This mantra was pretty well adhered to, and we were generally free of trouble.

One night, however, when Barrie was away and Terry Usher, the teacher, and I were manning the bar, someone looked like stirring up a team of shearers. I grabbed a bar stool and, holding it on high, I said, "Anyone who steps out of line will wear this stool".

It must have looked as if I meant business because everyone settled down.

A British journalist after a visit to the pub described me in an article:

Barrie's good-looking wife Lori plays the piano-accordion like an angel, but when trouble threatens in the bar she has been known to stand on the bar wielding a bottle and is said to have a punch like a steer.

He showed a bit of journalistic licence there I think. He also called me *the bottle-toting Lori*. The law allowing women to drink in public bars was only passed in 1965, just in time for our entry into the hotel business. It was a time of change when women were now allowed to drink in the main bar, but it seemed quite natural in Kynuna for women to do so, although most women used the Ladies Lounge if the bar was a bit busy and noisy. No sex discrimination there. Some of the women customers liked a game of pool on the table in the Lounge and enjoyed many an afternoon doing that while in town to pick up schoolchildren, often with our boys joining in. Steve liked to dress up like Eddie Charlton and emulate his persona. Our friend Edwina (Eddy) Naughton liked a game of pool and Barbara Howard, wife of a local grazier, also was a dab hand at this pastime. (Barbara and her husband, Jim, later bought the newsagency in Winton, which they ran for many years with their large family.)

After we were in the pub a couple of months, we decided to rename the old place. We reckoned that The Blue Heeler was topical and apt. The new name was chosen in honour of our blue cattle dog, Bull, given to Barrie by the Common Ranger, Vince Mahoney, in Julia Creek when Vince left town.

The Blue Heeler Hotel was duly registered on January 27, 1967. From then on we tried to have the name known all over Australia as the Outback pub famous for cold beer, great service, good food and conviviality. I think we were pretty successful and Barrie's gift for a gimmick was largely responsible for the good press we received. Some people said we wouldn't have become so well-known if Barrie's father, Ern, wasn't associated with the *QT*. Ern certainly gave us publicity, but I don't think the *QT* was ever that influential with regards to our business.

Business grew rapidly. If I was at a CWA meeting at the hall up the road and Barrie became snowed under with customers, some wanting food, he would hang a tea towel from our bedroom window, clear for all to see. I would then hotfoot it home to attend to the customers. It was always "business before pleasure".

A big part of our trade came from tourist buses. Early in the piece a bus was held up in Kynuna overnight because of wet roads following a storm. To keep the passengers amused, Barrie suggested I play them a tune on my piano-accordion. I did and my act was so popular we realised we'd hit upon a winning formula. The pub would become famous, not only for its cold drink and good food, but for entertainment.

So began our long practice of entertaining bus passengers, truckies and general patrons, with Barrie integrating his humour, singing and whipcracking into the show. We ended up with all sorts of props, hats and bits and pieces appropriate for the songs, kept under the bar.

People seemed to love writing about The Blue Heeler in newspaper and magazine articles. One tourist writing in a newspaper described the pub as: *The Wackiest Pub in the West.* Journalist Chris Black wrote: *Barrie Patrick is a sort of outback Paul Hogan, but three times funnier.* We weren't then aware of Paul Hogan, as TV still hadn't reached our neck of the woods, so it didn't mean much to us. Fortunately most reviews were complimentary but, as Father with his extensive newspaper experience said philosophically, "Any publicity is good publicity".

Barrie enjoyed playing the ocker. He relished wearing a Jacky Howe singlet or an old flannelette shirt and his vocabulary would reflect his mode of dress. He often referred to himself as Bazza the Bastard from the Bush and became famous for such bush wisdom as *Never trust a man in a Black Hat.*

One night, after the Kynuna races, Barrie rode Blondie Hall's grey mare, Blue Bonnet, into the bar, which caused much mirth and yahooing. We were told of an occasion before our time in the pub when Ron Teece, a local lad, rode a horse on to the front veranda. Unfortunately he miscalculated the entry spot and his head came into contact with a sharp piece of wrought-iron decoration and made a deep cut. Being a tough bushie, Ron declined a trip to the doctor and had someone stitch him up with horsehair and a household sewing needle and a touch of rum for a disinfectant and painkiller.

Barrie never missed an opportunity to entertain. I once bought him a pair of blue joggers for working behind the bar from Searle's shop in Winton, where you could buy just about anything for the male of the species. They were the first pair of sporty shoes Barrie had owned since the old sandshoe days. Barrie found them so comfortable to work in that he rang Mr Searle and ordered another pair of the same shoes to be sent on the next mail truck. Mr Searle said they only had red ones left in that size, but Barrie insisted, "Send them out, they'll do". Much to the amusement of tourists, he wore one of each colour, red on one foot, blue on the other. Anything to raise a few bob for the Flying Doctor.

By this time, we had started "passing the hat" around after our shows to fundraise for the Royal Flying Doctor Service. (There would be large and regular contributions to the RFDS until we left Kynuna.) The Flying Doctor Service is a virtual lifesaver. Sometimes you could get to hospital quicker via the Flying Doctor than would be possible for city folk by ambulance. No traffic jams up there in the sky. A very noble service.

The idea of changing the hat for a "pot" literally dropped out of the sky when the RFDS plane did a low sweep up the main street of town and the nurse dropped something out. Our kids raced up the road at the sight of a roll of toilet paper and something else flying through the air. They grabbed it and brought it into the bar. It was an old-fashioned enamel "gozunder" decorated with flowers and now somewhat dented from the hard landing on the bitumen. People from nearby McKinlay had given the bedroom chamber pot to the nurse as an engagement present and she had decided to donate it to Kynuna, with toilet paper included. Incidentally, another day a friend in a low-flying light aircraft said "Hello" by dropping a 2lb packet of flour at our front door.

From that day on, "the pot" was then taken around the customers when we were doing the show, usually for busloads of tourists and truckies. We raised many thousands of dollars in the old jerry-pot for "the Doctor". One happy night in later years when we had a bar full of truckies with no women around except me, Barrie and a mate decided to do a striptease as dared by the drinkers. They had to crawl along the length of the bar in the raw. The reward for this daring act was a donation to the pot for the Flying Doctor. They couldn't resist the dare and there was me, pumping out "The Strip Polka" on the piano-accordion (back turned of course) and the spectators cooey-ing like crazy. The pot collected $200 that night.

The Flying Doctor had a monthly clinic, or "Surgery", in the CWA hall, but the service was, and still is, on call 24 hours a day when needed. Clinics were usually for immunisations, script repeats, coughs, colds and all the ailments that country folk can usually put off until the next Flying Doctor visit. We had to call the Doc a few times, mainly for travellers.

The pilot would fly low over Kynuna to warn of their arrival. When the plane landed, someone would meet it, usually the policeman in his Toyota or Joe Lucas in his Land Cruiser ute, and would transport the doctor, nurse and pilot into town for the regular clinic. Someone always rode in the back of the ute, usually standing up, but no-one minded, it was all part of the process. Sometimes the Naughtons, who owned Kynuna Station where the airstrip was located, drove the crew across the Diamantina channels. One Flying Doctor day, a couple of our kids woke up feeling very off colour and we were able to get the Doc to call into the pub and diagnose the illness. It turned out to be hepatitis and affected our kids and some locals, the source tracked down to a bus driver who was held up at the pub for a couple of days by the weather. He'd said he wasn't well, but no-one had predicted the diagnosis. Joe's wife, Lukie, also succumbed. Barrie and I were lucky enough to avoid infection.

One doctor, Tim O'Leary, was a real character and a very popular doctor who served in the RFDS for many years. (In fact we never had a Flying Doctor who wasn't a popular figure and good at his job.) Sometimes in an emergency (in our pre-mobile-phone era), the pub would receive a call and someone would dash up to the hall to interrupt Tim's consultation and let him know the details. He'd then leave his doctor's room and call out to those waiting to see him. "Are any of you buggers dying?" he'd ask in his Irish brogue. If everyone answered in the negative he said, "Well I'll be off to see someone who is. See you next month".

On occasion, things could end badly. Once a busload of school children from Sydney pulled up at the pub and the driver reported they had a very sick girl on board. We contacted the Flying Doctor Service and because of the delay in getting to us they suggested that the bus carry on to McKinlay. They'd fly to McKinlay and from there transport the patient to Mount Isa. Unfortunately the young lass didn't make it. I believe she'd fallen ill before leaving Sydney, but hadn't told anyone because she didn't want to miss the trip. It was only in Winton that she said she was unwell. What a very sad trip for the other children.

During our time, Ian Robinson and David Cooke were also very popular and dedicated doctors. RFDS pilot John Murkin was not only a good pilot, but a dab hand as a carpenter. John, or Furkin Murkin as he called himself, was a real fun chap. On one flying visit he discovered that Harry Lamb, an elderly Kynuna chap, needed a pair of crutches. John got busy with his carpentry skills and, with the help of a local policeman, soon had them ready.

We always transported our own children by car to Julia Creek or Winton if an emergency occurred in the family, although the Flying Doctor did pierce both the girls' ears. To save time, they went in the truck with him to the airstrip and, while the King Air plane was warming up, had their ears done.

The Bold Gendarmes.

Barrie entertaining the patrons.

CHAPTER 15

Bus Coming!

It wasn't long before The Blue Heeler became a "must-see" destination on the tourist map. A coach or two, or six, often arrived at the pub midmorning, although many came in the late afternoon and pitched their tents on our spare allotment ready for a night of partying. When anyone saw it breast the hill to the east of us the call went out, "Bus coming!" It was everyone to his or her station, ready for the onslaught. Some tourists rushed to the bar to be first served, but most headed for the loos down the back. If there was a big queue, people of both sexes, but mostly men, would "go" in the prickly bush gully or behind the outbuildings. If the bus was loaded with schoolchildren and soft drinks were in demand, our kids' "stations" were busy.

Orders would start to come in for food and a list would be sent to the kitchen or called over the intercom, a later modern addition to the bar. The order might be for 20 hot dogs, 10 hamburgers, 10 pies, a cooked chook and sandwiches. The rush was on, usually with one of the kids rushing the orders out to the bar when they were ready. If there were more than one bus, as often happened, it was all the more fast and furious. Often the person's name or sandwich filling was attached to the paper wrapping, but confusion still sometimes reigned.

We often did smorgasbord meals, usually lunch, where we could be a bit more prepared. The bus driver would phone us from Winton or The Curry to order the meal, leaving us a couple of hours to get the food on the table. Still a bit of a rush.

When the people were asked to pay on their way into the dining room they often had some good excuses. On one occasion an elderly lady said her sister didn't want lunch, so she only paid for one. However, on looking at the amount of food on the plate, and the fact that she had surreptitiously picked up two plates, I became suspicious – surely one "oldish" lady couldn't eat all that! Anyway, once on the veranda, where most people were eating, I noticed they shared the one enormous pile between the two of them. They again stopped for lunch at The Heeler on their way back from Ayres Rock (now Uluru), but I was a wake-up, telling them they had to pay for two meals. I suppose they tried this trick at a lot of their stops.

We only had beds for about a dozen people, so the sleeping arrangements of the bus passengers was humorous when they were stuck at the pub in the Wet. Some slept in the bus and others took turns to sleep in the beds without bothering to change the sheets. Bus owner Jack McCafferty was a great supporter of ours, and if he accompanied a tour he'd make sure the passengers were all shouted a couple of drinks. Some bus passengers were too stingy to buy anything, so if no-one shouted they asked for glasses of water. This was quite irksome as it meant a lot more glasses to wash, for no profit. Having no mains power we didn't have a modern glass washer either. But you have to take the good with the bad.

Jack McCafferty had a wide variety of people from every walk of life on his tours. I remember one tour he had a group of nuns on board. They were very happy-go-lucky and played quoits in the bar. Jack always made sure that his passengers made a good contribution to the RFDS via "the pot".

After the customers were served, the crowd usually grew. There is nothing like a crowd to draw a crowd, and ours included truckies, motorists and locals pulling in to see what was going on. The bus driver would ask, "What about a singsong?" Out would come the piano-accordion from under the bar and Barrie would give his "Old Mare" spiel and the show would begin.

As well as singing a few songs with all the props from under the bar – hats, cymbals, baton, etcetera, Barrie did a bit of whipcracking, the chief trick being to crack a cigarette out of my fingers, or mouth occasionally, to the amazement of the crowd. He'd even flick a cap, previously undone, off a stubby as well. Barrie dressed in a police cap and waving a baton would sing "The Gendarme Song" and "I See the Moon, the Moon Sees Me" dressed in a Salvation Army style hat with cymbals. "The Green Beret" was very popular and sometimes truckie Kevin Russell, a good friend and customer, added sobbing actions to suit the song. The tourists loved it. Barrie also had a revolting old wig that caused quite a bit of mirth when he wore it.

While this was going on, we passed "the pot" around for the Flying Doctor and, if we had no other bar help, served customers as well! I often pulled beers while wearing a piano-accordion.

Barrie's repartee and quick wit played a large part in the popularity of the show. He was never at a loss for a quick retort. If someone asked him a personal question, he would say, "Nunya".

"What do you mean?" they'd ask.

"Nunya ya bloody business," he'd reply.

This and the old one about the colour of underpants I mentioned earlier were popular answers.

Traffic on the Landsborough Highway was sporadic and unpredictable and of course we had as many quiet days as hectic ones. In the holiday season we might do up to half-a-dozen shows – or gigs – during the course of a single day, and I turned down a few invitations to join a bus tour with my piano-accordion. This chance to see The Centre was very tempting, but it's a thing I still haven't done (but which I hope to rectify soon).

Barrie's brother, Don, joined us in the pub for a while where his cooking and musical skills were very much appreciated. His Cornish Pasties were especially in great demand. He also gave me a break with the piano-accordion when the tourists were partying in the pub. He was musically gifted and worked as pianist-singer at pubs and restaurants under the name "Rocky" Patrick. He entertained in Noosa restaurants for years and he continued this career after his marriage to Nanette Gibson in Townsville, a wedding we'd attended when we lived in Julia Creek.

One of Barrie's popular opening remarks was to ask a tourist where he or she came from. They'd invariably say Sydney or Melbourne and Barrie would then ask, "Who's got the pub in Melbourne these days?" Some fell for it and went on to say that it was a big town with plenty of pubs and Barrie would feign surprise. I guess some of them thought we were ignorant "Bushies". If they mentioned a plan to cross Bass Strait to go to Tasmania, Barrie would say, "I'm not going that way".

One tourist asked Barrie why he called Bull his blue cattle dog "Hind Here". He'd mistaken the order for the dog to come to heel for the dog's name. Another question asked occasionally was, "Why have all the trees been cut down? Why didn't the pioneers leave them like those on the riverbank?" We had to explain that there never were many trees on the western plains – that is the nature of the terrain.

We had a busload or three in the bar when one scholarly looking chappie from Melbourne, much taken with the mimosa bush in bloom, came in, unwrapped his pristine white handkerchief and showed us his "great find". He decided it would look good in his Victorian garden and had collected "seeds". He unwrapped what looked like a handful of little pebbles. Those of us who knew the difference between sheep dung and mimosa seeds were dumbstruck. Our pet lamb, Lambie, liked to rest, and to do other things, in the shade of the tree. We let the tourist go on his merry way in blissful ignorance. With any luck, maybe Lambie might have eaten some mimosa seeds and a mimosa tree grew in Melbourne after all.

A load of bus passengers usually meant a few more signatures and "souvenirs" on the walls. Hats were the most prolific, but pieces of ladies underwear were common adornments too. Barrie also had his favourite decorations – hats, whips, harnesses and ropes hanging from the walls, collecting dust. At one stage the Licensing Commission told us to get rid of all the signatures, so they had to be painted over. (I noticed on a trip to Kynuna years later that the walls were again covered with the names of people who had travelled that track.)

The overnight camping coaches were a lot of fun as well as a lot of work. They always had a cook on board, but some passengers wanted snacks in between meals or the cook wanted a break. They often set up their tables at the front of the pub and ate on the veranda. After the tents were set up and the tourists showered and fed, they would make for the bar and a big night usually followed, with the normal show. In those days, closing time was always 10pm, so we closed the doors at that time, but the crowd stayed on. As nearly everyone smoked, the atmosphere soon became thick as we soldiered on for a couple more hours. (I sometimes thought some of the cigarettes had a strange odour.)

We sold a number of souvenirs in the bar, including little bottles of Diamantina water from the Combo Waterhole. This waterhole is 20 kilometres east of Kynuna on the Winton road and is famous for the song "Waltzing Matilda". During visits there the kids filled a few wine flagons from the waterhole, which we decanted into the little labelled bottles. The swagman of that song is supposed to have jumped into the waterhole when the troopers were chasing him for sheep stealing. Banjo Paterson's original words say the swagman camped *in* a billabong, but I think *by* the billabong would have been more comfortable. Some people doubted that we were selling the real thing, but they were "ridgy-didge".

Kynuna local Richard Magoffin did a lot of research into the Waltzing Matilda story and published a book or two on the subject. A grazier, poet and author who lived on and owned a grazing property in the district, Richard had a lot of documentation to back up his story. His grandfather, Dick, had lived in the area and the family were friends of the MacPhersons, who owned Dagworth at the time of Paterson's visit. One night Richard brought his button-accordion into the bar with a copy of the original manuscript written by Christina Macpherson. He and I played and sang the words and the original tune for "Waltzing Matilda". Richard said it was the first-ever rendition of this original version in Kynuna.

In all my years west of Longreach, about 20 in fact, I only ever visited the Combo once, and that was late one evening when I took a phone message from the pub to someone having a fundraising evening by the billabong. With no mobile phones, all messages were delivered by hand.

At the end of a long night in the pub, we restocked the fridge and collapsed into bed. Then followed another day similar to the previous one. First job was to clean the pub out and cook breakfast for houseguests, some of whom stayed overnight because of the presence of the partying tour coach and its passengers. Washing the bed linen and cleaning the rooms also had to be done. It was always "up and at 'em" first thing in the morning to late at night!

On the squeeze box again.

The RFDS collection pot.

CHAPTER 16

King of the Road

During our 14 years in Kynuna we encountered many and varied situations as would be expected with such a variety of human beings on the premises at times. Some hilarious, some tragic, with a lot of just plain interesting in between.

A traveller arrived at the pub one day in 1968 when we, family and customers alike, were crowded around the transistor on the bar. We were listening to a fight broadcast from Tokyo between "Fighting Harada" and the Australian boxer Lionel Rose. The fight was the World Bantamweight Title, which Rose won. We were all absorbed in the broadcast when a strange-looking man walked through the door. For a moment we couldn't make out what was wrong with him. He had a peppered look on his face. He said, "I've shot myself".

He was driving from Winton to Kynuna through the Ayrshire Hills when he spotted emus near the road. Why he would want to shoot one, I can't fathom, but he stopped the car to get his shotgun out of the boot. The gun was apparently loaded, because the trigger got caught up with the strap of his camera, which hung around his neck, and it went off leaving him with a badly damaged hand and slightly damaged face. It would have been quicker for him to return to Winton rather than continue on for Kynuna. Of course he had to be transported to medical help. Fortunately his injuries weren't too serious – he was very lucky. He gave Barrie the 70-year-old shotgun with beautiful carvings on the metal stock. (We kept that gun until Australia tightened its gun laws in the wake of the Port Arthur massacre in 1996.)

Motorists often found themselves in trouble on the outback roads and not infrequently were averse to following advice given by locals, including police, local property owners and publicans. One chap walked miles into Kynuna after his car broke down on a hot, dry day that only the outback can produce. He walked into the bar and said, "The corrugations are bad". He had walked about 20 miles and we all expected him to ask for water, but his first comment was on the state of the road! He was extremely dehydrated. He had a meal, brought it all up and then lay in our kids swimming pool all afternoon. The pool by the way was half a galvanised iron tank, out on the lawn in the shade of the pub.

There was always traffic heading to or from Mount Isa and Darwin and cars weren't as reliable in those days. Often motorists in broken-down cars would implement a bush mechanic's method of repair. Chewed-up Minties or gum were thought to fix a leaking petrol tank, and Coca-Cola poured over battery terminals could make a reluctant vehicle start up. A broken fanbelt? Try ladies' panty hose. A lot of old cars ventured our way, often with people looking for a job and perhaps a better life in the outback. These were people who had limited resources, but were willing to try their luck.

Some Japanese motorcyclists found themselves bogged west of Kynuna and two locals rescued them and looked after them until the road reopened, and they came to the pub to stay. After they returned to Japan they sent some beautiful gifts to us all. I was given a lovely statue of a geisha girl, which I still have. One chap's father owned a big camera-manufacturing business in Japan and the gifts were very generous. They probably realised that if they hadn't been found they could have perished, or near to it.

Of course not everyone the locals helped was so generous, in fact the reverse was often the case. One family we helped, fed and sheltered in a Wet spell took all the sheets and towels and a couple of pillows from the room they had been staying in. I unsuccessfully tried to get them picked up by police further up the road. I later spoke to a truckie who helped them on the track, getting them out of a bog, and he said they showed him the linen they pinched from pubs and motels all along the road from Sydney. Some of it was even monogrammed.

On another odd occasion a tourist came into the bar and said he'd been bitten by a snake in the men's bathroom. We immediately became concerned, but he said he wasn't worried because "it was only about 30 cm long and too small to do any harm". He was more interested in having a laugh about the shower rose which, to make-do until we could get the proper fitting, was a large prune tin with nail holes in the bottom. We heard that the snakebite victim had to seek medical attention when he arrived in McKinlay, very unwell.

Travellers didn't always come by road. Occasionally a helicopter or a fixed-wing air-craft would stop at the pub and fuel up at our petrol bowser. The pilot would fill a four-gallon drum from the bowser and walk to the nearby machine to fuel up. I think it was the beginning of Duncan's interest in becoming a pilot, because once he flew in a helicopter that fuelled up at the pub.

We saw many shearing teams come and go when wool was fetching a reasonable price and in demand, and before some graziers changed their properties to cattle grazing. Some had both cattle and sheep. The shearers were good spenders and of course headed for the pub for a night out "occasionally". On cut-out day, they'd bring their cheques to be cashed, so we had to be well cashed-up to meet the demand. Shearing is hot, hard work and engenders in the workers a great thirst, and their custom was much appreciated. We had very little trouble and if two teams met at the bar we managed to keep a happy atmosphere. Of course there are always exceptions like the time I offered to sort them out with a bar stool held aloft. We thought it strange at the time that one shearer drank only Coca-Cola, but always seemed to be the first to get drunk. I realise now how hyped-up one can get on Coke if enough is drunk. A couple of chaps, who couldn't manage to keep control of their spending, gave us their money for safekeeping and claimed it only when leaving town. We kept their cash in a stubby cooler with their name on it, and took the money for the drinks from there.

There was an opal field south of Kynuna towards Middleton and optimistic miners would camp there, looking for a hoped-for bonanza. People had a habit of bringing rocks, valuable or otherwise, into the bar to be put on display. We had all sorts of stones, some containing opal or amethyst and quite a lot containing fossils and petrified wood. I never got to see that part of the country, although our kids were taken there by John Markwell, our good friend and local property owner, who was visiting a waterhole called Derry-Derry in the vicinity.

We had a large rock we called a thunder egg, which Barrie told the tourists was the Kynuna Surf Club football. (More on the Surf Club in a later chapter.) There was also a shallow Aboriginal Nardoo dish (that's what we called it anyway), with a pounding stone for crushing seeds for food. Alas one night, a drunk Winton man knocked over a gas cylinder and smashed the dish in two. We also had a good specimen of an Aboriginal axe, dug up near the petrol bowser when the McKinlay Shire Council was putting in kerb and channelling in front of the pub. One of the workers gave it to us and remarked that someone must have dropped his change, referring to the custom of barter of possessions among the native population many, many moons ago.

Among other things brought into the bar, one of the more unusual was an Esky containing several small crocodiles. The ringer who brought them from the Gulf was courting in Longreach at the time and thought he would surprise his lady-love with this unusual gift, but while showing us his "prize" someone knocked over the Esky, and we had crocodiles running all over the floor of the bar. They were supposed to be going to a swimming pool in Longreach and I suppose it would not be the only time crocs were illegally transported around the country in a car.

We had quite a few artists call in at the pub over the years. Once the Mornington Island Dance Group performed for us on the lawn. They sold us some of their costumes, including the conical hat covered in human hair and pink and grey galah feathers, which took the pride of place in the bar. Ted Egan, the folk musician, joined in with an impromptu session with us a couple of times with his beer carton for percussion and Aboriginal actor David Gulpilil did emu and kangaroo dances when he called in for petrol on his way home to the Gulf for a rest after an acting engagement. A group of Balinese dancers called at the pub once, all beautiful and touring under the auspices of the Arts Council. We also had a visit from an Anglican Bishop, John Lewis, who played the guitar and had an attempt at whipcracking out in front of the pub. Our local Anglican bloke sometimes got behind the bar, dog collar and all. The tourists loved it.

One year a group of men arrived with a light aircraft to conduct an aerial mineral survey of the hills south of Kynuna. They were booked into the hotel and we provided their board and lodgings for the duration, the trade being welcome. Unfortunately the plane crashed, bringing the operation to a standstill. Luckily no-one was seriously injured.

Truckies were our biggest customer base and most reliable, after the locals. We were always glad to see a "semi" coming over the hill and the sound of the air brakes was a welcome one. "Lights on the Hill", "Trumby" and other Slim Dusty songs were popular at The Blue Heeler.

One afternoon when big storms came up out of the blue, several semis loaded with cattle from a property near the head of the Diamantina reached Kynuna, but couldn't go any further. This was a regular occurrence after big rain. The roads were wet and boggy and plans to unload the cattle had to wait until daylight. What a night! Cattle stamping and bellowing in the trucks all night right outside our bedroom window, and truckies camped all over the front veranda! None of us had much sleep. When daylight came, the trucks went to the rodeo yards and the cattle were unloaded. They were then grazed on the common by a couple of local horsemen until the road was passable. It was a busy time in the pub with other trucks carrying general loads to Mount Isa and Darwin and a McCafferty's busload of tourists also stranded by the same storm. Once it rained, *nothing* moved! The bitumen road from Winton to Cloncurry was a missing link for many years. Sometimes there were no signs of a storm, but by the time the vehicles traversed the dirt roads to Kynuna, a two-and-a-half hour trip from Winton, the road could be impassable.

When it looked as if we'd be cut off from the rest of the world for a while, truckie Jimmy Gamble, a good friend of ours, left his truck and two trailers at our front door near the old rain tree and went home to Toowoomba. The rain came with a vengeance and Barrie thought it would be a good idea to move the truck in case the Diamantina overflowed. He put the proposition to Steven, our eldest, who said, "Yes, I can move it, Dad". Steve started it up and after a while got it moving by rocking it back and forward on the wet ground. He drove it on to our spare allotment on the top, western side of the pub. He made a wide sweep and did a U-ie, bringing the truck back to within a few metres of the building, sure that it would be safe there. However, the flood was bigger than expected and the water ended up reaching the big step tank, but the load was still out of water. The truck stayed there for a few weeks until the roads dried out and Jimmy reclaimed it. He was very pleased with the job Steve had done.

Jimmy was a great character, and if stuck at the pub during rain would do a few comical things to keep the stranded travellers happy, including going down the bar in the nude! Once he had everyone in stitches, standing in the bar and reading "the Bible" in a slow stentorian tone. He actually had a western paperback in his hand, but he seemed to know quite a bit about the sacred Book. Having a comedian in residence helped travellers pass the long days of doing nothing. In addition to Barrie, that is.

Sometimes truckies had a dog travelling in the cab with them. One day a big bull terrier and one of our dogs got into a tussle and were having a ding-dong battle under the front veranda. A truckie crawled under the floorboards and successfully broke up the fight. We were amazed at this effort and remarked on his bravery. He said he wasn't frightened of the dogs, but all the spiders lurking there gave him the heebie-jeebies! Once a huge snake fell from the undercarriage of a semi-trailer and headed for safety beneath our front veranda. It was quickly dispatched.

We only had a certain number of bar stools, and when the bar was crowded some people were lucky to get a seat, and others weren't. Many sat on the edge of the veranda. A truckie who was one of the lucky ones wasn't going to risk losing his seat so he took his bar stool with him when he went down the back to the Gents!

During our time at the pub, Mary Kathleen mine was productive and quite of lot of uranium passed our way on semi-trailers, thus increasing the trucking traffic and helping our business. We had a couple of pieces of the ore on the shelf behind the bar with all the other rock specimens.

Dust was a major irritant owing to the dry, dusty plains and roads, with traffic, especially semi-trailers, dragging a pile of dirt into town on their wheel rims. I was washing our first brand-new vehicle, a Holden ute, when a "new" truckie came roaring into town with all his dust flying. Of course the wet vehicle was instantly covered in mud. I blew my top and explained to him that courteous drivers idled into town to let the dust settle and fall off the wheels before they pulled up. The poor "newie" was very apologetic and we later became good friends, a condition we shared with numerous truckies over the years at Kynuna. They were very good spenders, most of them, and very loyal. Of course we tried to look after them at our pub, their home-away-from-home.

It was an unfortunate reality that we also had our share of trouble from passers-by. Our children became very astute at picking up on the "no-hopers" who traversed the western roads, usually to get away from some crime down south or up north in the Northern Territory. They'd say things like, "I think that bloke over there is a crim. Things don't look right with their vehicle", and they were usually right. They could pick them a mile off. An inbuilt trait? Barrie certainly had it. If we thought it was merited, we'd phone the next police station and have the suspects checked out. We had a lot of "crims" pass our way over the years.

One very important and necessary position in a country town is that of the policeman. We had a number of these enforcers of the law over the years. Another very important, in fact vital, person in a small town is the postmaster (or mistress).They helped keep us in touch with the outside world. Cedric Crabbe, who everybody called Muddy, was a much-loved postmaster in our time. The postmaster was also the telephonist and would have been extremely busy, as it was a 24-hour a day exchange. Our phone number was Kynuna 8. Another of the postmaster's jobs was sorting, receiving and dispatching the mail for each of the three services we had weekly. When Muddy died we had a plaque made in his honour and placed on the wall behind the bar.

During one big Wet, one of our motors broke down and Edwina Naughton, the President of the CWA, Kynuna Station owner and dear friend, kindly lent us the Southern Cross motor from the hall. Without it we couldn't have kept the food edible and the town was packed with stranded motorists. Joe Lucas, who could turn his hand to most things, with another mechanic stuck in town, installed the big motor and we were back in business. A couple of CWA members disagreed with Edwina's decision, but "them's the breaks". We donated a gas stovette in appreciation. It came in handy for afternoon teas when there was a meeting in the hall as it saved lighting the CWA wood stove for a cuppa.

A while after this I was woken about 6am by someone banging on the bedroom wall, wanting petrol. To keep them quiet and get them out of our hair I rose and served them. They didn't sound too grateful and raved on about the cost of petrol. I said if Labor Prime Minister Gough Whitlam hadn't removed the subsidy, petrol would be a lot cheaper in the West. They went on about Malcolm Fraser being Prime Minister long enough to reinstate it. (By the way, there was a big celebration in the bar when Gough was deposed – truckies and graziers alike.) Anyway, these travellers headed off in the direction of Mount Isa without giving any thanks. Apparently if you have a bowser you are supposed to man it 24 hours a day! That afternoon we had a CWA meeting and when we went to make afternoon tea we discovered that the gas stove was missing. Then we found the pillow and bedding from the Flying Doctor couch had also gone. I remembered seeing a pillow in the back of the vehicle when I had fuelled up, and thought at the time, that looks out of place. We also found signs of people having slept in the hall. They had broken in and helped themselves! Our policeman was out of town, so Barrie rang the police at The Curry and The Isa, but the suspects had a head start of about eight hours and made it over the border into the Northern Territory and out of the jurisdiction of the Queensland Police.

We would sometimes fill a car with petrol in the middle of the night. Ignoring them at 2am was sometimes not a wise option. When this happened, one of us worked the bowser and the other stood on a closed-in part of the pub veranda holding a loaded shotgun, in case the customers had mischief on their minds. I can't recall any "drive-offs" at the bowser, but we didn't give anyone the chance. If someone pulled up and started to fill their petrol tank without asking us first, we turned the power off from behind the bar, thus ensuring that if they wanted "juice" they had to be served by one of us. It is inadvisable to travel those roads without filling up when possible and to run out of petrol could lead to disaster.

Once when Barrie was "checking the perimeter", a nightly chore, he saw some fellows with a fire burning near one of the buildings, cooking pieces of pumpkin they stole from a bag at the side of the pub. We approached them to enquire why they had lit the fire near our premises, and one of them came at us with a speargun, looking as if he meant business. Barrie always carried his revolver when checking the premises out at night (a .22 calibre Smith and Wesson), but I don't think he ever drew it. As on this occasion, he could usually talk the miscreants into leaving the premises quietly.

Another night when Barrie was doing his rounds he came in and said a car belonging to a Winton man we knew quite well was parked around the other side of the old quarters with a few young fellows asleep in it. We called the policeman, who rounded them up. They were a bit stunned after the shock of being woken up and didn't put up too much resistance. The Winton man was pleased to get his car back.

Another time we had a gun-waving chap in the town wandering around the ridges, and we were really worried. There was no policeman in town, and Barrie put Joe Lucas on standby and went and accosted the man. He had a car and no money to pay for petrol, so Barrie took the gun (a .303 rifle), filled his car up in exchange for it, and sent him on his way. Strangely he drove to Winton, then doubled back heading in the direction of Mount Isa, but we never came across him again, although one of our friends saw him in Mount Isa a day or two later. (That rifle also went the way of our other firearms when the Government changed the gun laws.)

I can't remember all the gun episodes, although someone told me recently he heard Barrie walked out to tourist buses with a shotgun and warned the driver that the passengers must be on their best behaviour, and if they didn't agree they wouldn't be allowed off the bus. Barrie did occasionally do some outrageous things and I believe this trick was at the behest of the coach captain.

Once a strange couple booked into one of the rooms and we noticed the man (naked) waving a .22 rifle around. We phoned our local policeman who very skilfully disarmed the chap and sent the couple on their way. I think the heat gets to travellers at times and makes them do strange things. On one express coach out of Kynuna, a woman passenger made a stir when the other passengers realised she had durex tape all over her face. She thought she'd found a cure for wrinkles!

On another occasion there was a big hunt in the district for a notorious criminal wanted for murdering someone on the wharves in Sydney. We were shown a photo of him and some of the people in the bar, including Barrie and Terry Fitzgerald, the dingo trapper, said they had seen him in the pub the day before. He had caused some of the drinkers to be suspicious of him because he said he had walked a long way, but his dress and appearance seemed to contradict that statement, and Barrie and Terry thought it obvious he'd arrived by some sort of vehicular transport. The police told Barrie to keep his revolver under the counter, as this fellow was wanted for murder. Of course we were very apprehensive while every property and shed in the district was checked. But the bird had flown. He must have headed back to Sydney as we later heard that someone had "knocked him off" down there.

One night when I was in charge of the hotel a few of what I considered as "undesirables" booked in. I was too nervous to turn them away so showed them to their rooms. The only person left in the bar was the local Catholic priest who was booked in as well. He said: "Don't worry, Lori, you'll be right. My father had a pub and I know how to be a 'chucker-outer'". I retired for the night feeling relieved, thinking, if a priest couldn't keep me safe, who could? I have the Lord on my side.

When they departed, those travellers left the bedroom walls and cot smeared with baby faeces. Luckily such experiences were rare.

We too travelled the surrounding roads often, usually to pick up supplies. We bought all our soft drinks from local manufacturers – Jumbo Harris in Julia Creek and George Steadman in Winton. We returned what bottles we could to those factories, beer stubbies preferred, and if we went to either town would take a trailer-load of empties and return with a load of full ones. The trip home from Winton was always an uncomfortable journey in the late afternoon with the sun slowly sinking in the west and into your vision, and passing traffic creating a great "dust storm".

One day I was forced to pull up to answer a call of nature. I stepped out on the driver's side and did the job. On getting back in the car, the 1964 Holden station wagon wouldn't start. I was stuck in the middle of nowhere with a car that wouldn't go. A fellow pulled up to assist when he saw the bonnet of the car up. Between the two of us we got the car going and I headed for home. There wasn't a lot of traffic on the highway in those days, and the sight of a Good Samaritan was most welcome. Deb was in the front seat and kept asking weepily, "When will we get home?" She was worried as something had also gone wrong with the back axle and it was a very slow trip.

On another trip to Julia Creek with a load of empties, the spare tyre on the drawbar of the trailer came loose and went bouncing along in the long grass at great speed. I spent about half an hour in the hot outback sun with flies for company as I looked for the darned thing. I eventually found it about 200 metres in front of me. It would be foolhardy to tow a trailer anywhere without a spare tyre, but especially in the West.

After he retired, our right-hand man Joe sometimes accompanied me on a trip to town, and his being on fluid tablets meant I often had to stop more than once for his convenience. You always had to look each way before carrying out the deed, and you could see the dust of a vehicle for miles, so had plenty of warning. One old drover told us of the night he left his missus by the side of the road. She also had stepped out of the car to do what she had to, but the door slammed shut and her old man took off. After going a few miles he thought her silence a bit uncharacteristic. He was talking to her without response. "What's up with you, woman, you're very quiet?" he asked. What he thought was the wife was the dogs in the back of the ute – he'd left her *miles* behind.

The diminution of place names is very common in the West. We would refer to The Curry, The Creek, The Isa and The

Heeler most times. When Eva and Ern were holidaying with us, I took them and Deb to The Isa for an overnighter. My in-laws were very amused by a sign on a sheet of corrugated iron they saw between McKinlay and The Curry saying "Lift-im-foot", a warning that there was a hazard ahead. When we reached The Isa we called in to see Curly Dann, a friend who had a sports store. He insisted we take a stuffed Johnson (freshwater) crocodile back to the pub to put on display. It was a bit over six feet long and originated in the Gulf of Carpentaria. We loaded the croc into the back of the station wagon, with his head over the top of the back seat, between Deb and Father. Unfortunately, owing to the corrugated roads, the old croc kept shifting, hitting Father in the side of the neck with his large teeth. When we got back to Kynuna, Father was bleeding. When asked what had happened, he truthfully replied that he'd been bitten by a crocodile.

The croc took pride of place high on the wall behind the bar. We could have kept him when we eventually left the pub, but Curly said if we didn't want to take him with us to leave him there and he'd collect him sometime. Many years later, he was still hanging there.

When the roads weren't dusty they were usually muddy and boggy and often brought traffic to a standstill. One thing you could bank on – they were always rough! After the first pub vehicle, the old Chev, we had an old grey Holden ute, bought from a destitute traveller. Once I took the kids into Julia Creek for a Christmas tree party in that ute and hit a big hole in the road just out of Julia Creek. I must have damaged the steering because when I went to do a right-hand turn into Jumbo Harris' yard I had no steering. A pin or something had come out of the steering mechanism, so we were lucky it happened so close to our destination. It could have been disastrous.

We gradually worked our way up the ladder of motor-vehicle prestige. Our next car was a '64 Holden station wagon bought from a friend in Longreach, then a new white Holden ute, and then the crème de la crème, the Toyota Land Cruiser station wagon.

I'll close this chapter with a poem written by Ern Patrick
after one of his visits to the pub. Like Barrie, Ern was
something of a poet of no mean ability. He later entered the
poem, which reflected our life between Culladar and The Blue
Heeler, in a competition. It eventually appeared in the *Bronze
Swagman Book of Bush Verse (1972)*:

CULLADAR

I know a place that is wide and free
Where the breezes sigh in the athel tree,
'Neath cloudless skies that save their stars
Like jewels at night for the coolibahs.

Where kangaroos roam and emus play
In air so crisp at the break of day;
Where Johnnie the dog impatiently waits
For his master to ride through the swinging gates.

Then it's off to work on the wind-swept plain,
With Johnnie and Barrie together again;
The mill at the ten-mile needs repair
And there are other jobs to do out there.

Oh, a ringer's life is a healthy one,
And he sings to the sky as he heads for home –
With a hunger keen and a king-sized thirst,
But the dogs must all be satisfied first.

When the "killer" is butchered and safe in the fridge,
He gazes out towards the ridge;
Could rain this week he muses and sighs
As he slaps the dust from his aching thighs.

On the morrow, he knows, he must get those sheep
Before the channels run fast and deep –
The stragglers all that missed the shear,
There seemed to be more of them this dry year.

So he settles down on the steps to gaze

At the rainbow sunset through the haze,
And the roast in the oven smells so good –
"No time for the big smoke's fancy food!"

Away from the city that gave him birth,
He smiles as he looks at the dark brown earth –
He's a better man *for sure, by far,*
For the years he spent at Culladar.

The girl he married was governess
And the pair of them coped with the droughty west –
He as ringer, stockman, inspector too,
She as everything else bar jillaroo.

But where are they now? Aye, there's the rub –
Mine hosts of a famous western pub.
And they smile as they serve behind the bar
And think of their days at Culladar.

The preacher's hat.

James Barrie Patrick and 'Bull'.

CHAPTER 17

Outback Kids

The back country, as it's known in the West, provides children with a very wide education in life. They live a completely different lifestyle from city kids, naturally, and learn many of life's idiosyncrasies and a lot of practical knowledge on their way through. As I mentioned earlier, the kids learnt to drive at a young age. To give them more education in that regard we would take them up to the racecourse to drive round and round the track. They were lucky too that some truckies taught them to drive their semis, and they became quite adept and knowledgeable by the time they went off to high school at Ipswich State High, boarding with the senior Patricks.

Our kids also gathered a lot of knowledge of the hospitality industry. The biggest rush of coach tours happened during the school holidays, when it was all hands on deck. One boy "manned" the bowser, as coaches attracted traffic. Motorists needing fuel for themselves as well as their cars pulled in. (Our fuel was supplied by a tanker from Julia Creek.) One boy kept the cold-room shelves stocked and Deb ran the food from the kitchen to the bar. In between times they collected glasses and cleaned tables. They were never really pleased at having to spend their "time off" working, but knew it was all part and parcel of living in a bush pub. Sometimes we had half-a-dozen buses in at a time. Bedlam!! A lot of the coachloads included children on holidays, and our kids thought it wasn't fair having to work while others were having a good time.

Steven started at Kynuna School as soon as we arrived and Duncan began the following year. The school had a pretty healthy enrolment in the '60s and early '70s with children from some 10 families in attendance. Kynuna School competed in sports days in McKinlay, Julia Creek and at the Mount Campbell Station school. They were much anticipated with uniforms, march-pasts, ribbons and trophies. All the schools from the shire gathered to compete. Small events, but very satisfying and beneficial to the education of the outback kids. Correspondence school pupils also competed.

Deb won most of the events in athletics for her age group. I remember seeing her win the 800-metre race in Julia Creek. She was so white and distressed that I was in tears, caused as much by pride in her tenacity and staying-power as her athleticism. Sometimes we would let her out of the car a couple of miles from the pub to run home. (She still seems to enjoy sport and in recent years has been competing in triathlons.) Barrie always admired Deb's swimming ability and style. He said she could have been a champion given the right training and opportunities.

One sports day a storm blew up between Julia Creek and Kynuna. I was driving the Toyota 4WD with Edwina Naughton and her boys on board as well as our "athletes". We had an awful trip home. I had never driven in four-wheel-drive or in the mud before because we stayed at home if rain looked imminent. Anyway, following the instructions of some of my passengers, I put the vehicle into four-wheel-drive and ploughed along, at one stage going into a 360-degree spin. I stopped on a grid and Jonathon Naughton got out, found a steel picket nearby and proceeded to clean the mud from around the wheels. The mud was so impacted around the tyres that it was difficult to make any progress. We got going again with all the other parents passing us in their conventional vehicles and I finally woke up that I'd be better off driving in two-wheel-drive. We eventually arrived home. The other drivers were obviously more skilled in the mud than I was. Not surprising I suppose, as they'd probably spent their whole lives in the bush. I learnt a lot about four-wheel-driving that day.

An easier trip to the Julia Creek Sports Day one year was in Brian Naughton's light aircraft. On recalling that flight I think I was brave to go flying with Brian, as he hadn't long learnt to fly and I hate heights, but I guess I just went with the flow. He related a story about nearly running out of fuel on one trip and having to make an emergency landing on a station road. He had some stockmen on board from Riversleigh Station in the Gulf and was taking them to Kynuna Station to help with a muster. Upon checking, he found the cap was off the petrol tank, and his passengers said, "Yes, boss, we saw something flying out of that hole".

The teachers were an asset to Kynuna. They did a great job with sometimes more than 20 pupils scattered through different year levels and with no teacher-aid, yardman or cleaner to help. We had a deal going with most of the teachers. We would give them an evening meal in exchange for a bit of night barwork. It was advantageous to all parties. I think the outback experience gained by these young men was invaluable and stood them in good stead when they returned to their coastal posts. Some had never been out of the big cities and were surprised and happy with the life experience gained in the West. Female teachers seemed less likely to be sent that far west. A lot of young people think it is the worst possible transfer, but I am sure that a spell west of the Great Divide contributes greatly to their life skills. Two of ours and the kids' favourites, Maurice Awhy and Peter Ralph, say the time spent in the West is something they still cherish. They never regretted the transfer.

School holidays were never a problem out West. The children were kept busy helping in the business, visiting their friends on a station or, for the boys, honing their skills on their air rifles with a bit of target practice. They got their first air rifles at about 10 and 12 years of age. This was considered a fairly normal ascension in their manly development. Barrie bought the rifles from Searle's Menswear. The kids loved testing their skills and practised on soft drink cans on fence posts. I don't think the air guns were detrimental to their upbringing and were a good test of accuracy, skill and concentration. Of course, when the new gun laws came in the rifles had to be destroyed, another link with the old days shattered, especially when Steven's gun had to go.

Entertainment for the children in the district was a bit scarce, but we held some events for them. At one stage we showed movies, courtesy of the school movie projector, at the pub, on the lawn or in the Ladies Lounge. But someone thought it was bad for the children to have it in the pub, although they always hung around while their parents had a "couple" anyway. The result was the pictures were moved to the CWA hall. This lowered the attendance, as some people would rather "have a few" than go up to the hall to see the pictures. There was a fancy dress dance for the kids once or twice while we were in Kynuna, as well as the Christmas tree nights.

We eventually got a small second-hand portable swimming pool with an electric pump. It was an improvement on the half-galvanised iron tank. And a very popular place on a hot day, too.

A funny outdoor evening was one Guy Fawkes night when some of the kids around town had accumulated a good pile of fireworks. They decided to pool them and let them off on our spare allotment on the western side of the pub. Barrie took control, and with all the youngsters standing around in their dressing gowns, started the show. First of all he gave a lecture on the dangers of crackers and had them all stand back. Unfortunately, one "bunger" jumped into the carton of assorted fireworks, and of course the whole lot went up in one great explosion. There were bungers and Catherine wheels going off in all directions and children running hell, west and crooked. They got a great laugh at Barrie's expense, but agreed it was unfortunate but necessary to terminate the show. Barrie took them inside and shouted them a lemonade each. I can't recall another Guy Fawkes night. That was probably because the Government made it illegal for the ordinary Tom, Dick or Harry to purchase or use fireworks without a permit. In Queensland, anyway.

One good thing about living in the isolated hamlets of the West is the amount of reading the children do. With no TV and half the time no-one to play with, books became a useful pastime for our kids, a habit they carried on into their adult years. Every time I went to town I bought books for them and the grandparents often gave them children's novels, which I think helped in their overall education.

If we were having a quiet Sunday night sometimes we had a barbecue down the back, cooking in our big, authentic camp oven given to Barrie by a drover in years gone by. We had a campfire singalong and played a few tapes. It was a nice change to our routine, sitting by a fire of gidgee coals on a clear western evening. I didn't like the menu the night they cooked a goanna over the fire, though. Slim Dusty and Ted Egan records and tapes were popular in the West, and Barrie and a mate, often truckie Sel Watkins, would play them by the hour (after hours), much to my chagrin if I was trying to sleep in the nearby bedroom.

Of course living in a bush pub was an education in itself. Our kids learnt a lot from the truckies, drovers, local and travelling horsemen and women and nearby station owners. Once when the rough riders were resting up in Kynuna, before competing in The Curry and The Isa rodeos, they gave Deb a horse to ride. I almost had a fit when she came racing up from the cattle yards, past the pub, full speed ahead, blonde hair flying in the breeze, accompanied by a few of the rough riders. I was expecting disaster, but she managed to stay on and stopped the wild ride. Shades of my own childhood. Deb was always up for any job suggested to her. Once Joe Lucas offered to show her how to castrate a pig when we had a litter in our sty. She came good and handled the operation with aplomb.

Steven, Duncan and Deb rode out with the drovers sometimes and enjoyed their company and the experience. If the drovers were too far from town when a cow calved, they would carry the baby calves on their chuckwagon, which also carried all their gear, and put the calves on the ground when they camped at night, so they could get a feed from their mothers. If the mother disowned the calf it was sometimes given to Duncan to take home and rear. There was a bit of competition for these little ones, but Duncan got lucky at times, much to the disgust of one local. Some thought that they were to be given all the poddy calves, as by divine right. We bought powdered milk by the large bag, and the calves were fed the same milk as us humans.

Our kids learnt a lot from the drovers and improved their horseriding skills as well. The sight of a big mob of cattle following the stock route across the common was very impressive. But now Barrie didn't have to "scratch for ticks" – he was serving beer instead. We had a few head of cattle over the years. Our brand was P2L. Barrie said one for Patrick and two for Lori.

Duncan had an affinity with all creatures. He took in and fostered a baby emu we called Demu. (When it got bigger Demu went off with a friend of ours.) Another of his many orphans was the aforementioned Lambie. The lamb was a bit of a nuisance at times. He'd go into our bedroom and seeing himself in the long wardrobe mirror would challenge what he thought was another lamb trying to take over his patch. It's a wonder he didn't break the 80-year-old mirror. The lamb also had a liking for potato chips. If a customer was eating a packet of chips, Lambie would do everything in his power to get it, eat the contents, leave the packet on the floor and walk off.

Eventually Lambie became too big a problem, sometimes knocking over children in his rush to get their salt and vinegars, so we sent him to Glenagra for our good friends John and Glenda Markwell to integrate with their station herds. He liked lying under the trees with their dogs for a start. He had become used to our dogs in the pub and thought *he* was a dog.

He eventually went off with a mob of sheep, but whenever John and his children went to inspect the flock they would take a packet of chips with them, rattle the paper and Lambie would come racing out of the herd looking for his favourite snack. It was the only way to tell him from all the other weaners since, to my mind, all sheep look alike.

We had a few odd events involving animals while at The Blue Heeler including a big calf belonging to Shirley the storekeeper that ate the washing off our line. I vividly remember that it chewed up a much-loved linen tablecloth of mine. The same animal once got locked in a guest bedroom for a couple of days. You can imagine the mess. Another time we lost a bitch for a few days, and eventually discovered her under the old quarters with a new litter of pups. How she got there was a bit of a mystery as there was only a small gap in the floorboards.

When bathing Steven one night I noticed he had a big lump on the outside of his hand – up from his little finger. When I asked him what happened, he said a couple of days earlier he and Duncan were boxing and when he went to hit his little brother he hit the end of our bed instead. It was obvious it was broken and needed treatment. Ken Jackson, a local lad, was going to Julia Creek so Steve and I cadged a ride to see Dr Wilson. Before we left, Barrie said, "Make sure the Doc knows what he's doing". He said that he'd seen many badly set bones in the bush, especially with stockmen. It put me in a very awkward position because when I queried the doctor about his skill he reached for the phone and asked if I wanted to talk to his ex-superior. Of course I said no and was very embarrassed, but I usually did as Barrie asked. The repair went well and Steven had a night in the Julia Creek Hospital.

We also had a bad experience when Steven suffered a severe asthma attack and Barrie set off with him to Winton. The poor kid was struggling for breath and as showers had fallen, the roads were bad. Barrie bogged the car a couple of times and passing truckies helped him out. He was very relieved to reach Dr Tony Fleming, another doctor in whom we had a lot of faith.

Another misadventure was caused by the daughter of a local customer who claimed to be a Tahitian Princess. She speared Deb in the foot with a garden fork while playing outside the pub with our kids. Deb also broke her nose while speeding around the beer garden of the North Gregory Hotel in Winton on another child's pushbike. A girl always on the go, Deb was a venturesome one.

Barrie often had some words of wisdom to dispense, especially to our kids. "Be honest, help your mate and fight a good round if you have to – but only if you have to – and if you have to, DON'T BLOODY MISS." I don't know if this was good advice or not, but it does cast light on Barrie's personality – always ready with a quick retort and full of innovative ideas.

After having our planned three children, we thought we'd done our bit for the country, but in the August school holidays of 1970, Steven, Duncan and Deb went to Mount Isa to holiday with our friends the Crane family who had a fruit business there. They were giving me a break as I was still recovering my health from a burst ulcer.

I had suffered pain for some time and became extremely unwell after competing in a gymkhana in early 1970. The last straw was the woodchopping! I decided I needed a break in Ipswich with family. The bus I travelled on stopped in Toowoomba for lunch, and after feeling unwell for the whole trip I decided to go to the Ladies, access to which was a spiral staircase. I passed out and the next thing I knew there were two large ambulance officers on the scene. Upon coming around, I made a dash for the handbasin and out spurted copious amounts of blood. I was taken to Toowoomba General Hospital where I spent weeks recuperating from a burst, large, shallow gastric ulcer. I was very annoyed about spoiling my new shoes and jumper, not only from the bloodstains, but also the nurse's scissors. When the coach arrived in Ipswich my in-laws were shocked when the driver said, "She's in the Toowoomba

Hospital". My sister, Barbara, rushed in from Pittsworth where she was living. Prior to this life-threatening event I had consulted several doctors who couldn't provide a diagnosis, so it was fortuitous that I happened to be in a city where I could get medical attention quickly.

Anyway, it was the first time the children had all been away together without parents and we must have enjoyed their absence – sometime later I found I was again with child.

However would I manage? It seemed an unassailable mountain to climb. I felt I was stretched to the limit already with three children and a pub. We were even bottling our own draught beer from the keg about then, making extra work.

I don't remember any morning sickness. No time I suppose!

While I was pregnant, Barrie was away from the pub one day when three fellows pulled in for petrol. I served them and against my better judgement pulled them a beer each, although it was not quite opening time. I felt sorry for them travelling in the summer heat. When I asked them for the money they took off. I raced for the phone, but owing to the fact that I had just mopped behind the bar and the vinyl-covered floor was wet, I landed on my rear when my feet went from under me. I immediately thought it could have harmed the unborn baby. I rang the local police station and the officer said he'd ring the McKinlay police station and alert them. They didn't catch the thieves and we were down a tank of petrol and three pots of beer, but thankfully the baby suffered no ill effects.

In March 1971 I decided I should pay a visit to our Winton doctor, Barry Wilson, with an overnighter to suit the bus timetable. The night before I left the pub we looked at the sky and said, "Mackerel Sky, rain coming, better get the visit to the Doc over and done with".

All was fine with the pregnancy and the next morning when I was about to return home, Barrie rang. "We had 10 inches of rain overnight. You won't be able to get back."

So began a long holiday in Winton. Every time I considered the roads dry enough to make a trip there'd be another dump of up to 10 inches of rain. There were three big falls during this period and the roads remained impassable. Finally Dr Wilson said not to go home in case I was caught in Kynuna when labour started.

While I was living at the North Gregory Hotel awaiting the birth, I was invited to go with a crew from BBC television to Rangelands station near Winton and watch the making of a film. It was a re-enactment of the Shearers' Strike of 1894, with the union shearers burning down the Dagworth shearing shed and leading to Banjo Paterson writing "Waltzing Matilda" in January 1895. Richard Magoffin played the part of the leader of the shearers. As I was pregnant I just sat up in the hills under a tree and watched the activity from afar. I had a good vantage spot and enjoyed the day's activities. On a more dramatic note, back at The Heeler, a traveller for some unknown reason fired shots at the pub in the middle of the night, one bullet hitting the petrol bowser and one the building. Fortunately no-one was hurt.

After 10 weeks in Winton, the local shop people remarked that it was the only 12-month pregnancy they had ever seen. They must have been sick of the sight of me and my long walks every day. Being away from the business for so long was a worry to me, but unavoidable in the circumstances, and I did enjoy the holiday, although a tad guiltily. Luckily, Barrie's parents were at The Heeler to lend a hand.

Winton is a very friendly town and people were kind to me, especially the Head family. I always called in to talk to the people in the shops, including Margaret (Emma) Gillies and Raine Gillies. Dr Wilson often drove past me on my walks, giving me a wave and telling me I was doing a good job by getting plenty of exercise. (Sadly, Dr Barrie Wilson, who also did a lot exercise including jogging and swimming, would die from a heart attack while swimming in the local pool in August 1973. In time, Mr Wally Rae opened the Dr Barry Wilson Memorial Park across the road from the swimming pool in his honour. Barry Wilson had tended the sick of Winton for about three years. Since he'd been our GP in Julia Creek before he relocated to Winton and had always been there when our family required the services of a good and trusted doctor, we were extremely sorry to learn that his life had been cut short.)

On May 25, 1971, after a six-hour labour, our new baby daughter made her appearance. Right from the start she could draw a crowd. It was the 4pm staff changeover when she arrived so both shifts of nurses were there to see her come into the world. Dr Wilson said, "You have a lovely little girl". Little? She was a shade under 10 pound (4½ kg) and 59½ cm long.

Dr Wilson rang the new father to give him the news, and by the time I was wheelchaired to my room, a telegram boy was handing me messages from the Kynuna populace. Barrie had immediately told the kids that they had a new sister and they took off and spread the news to every house. The locals all phoned the post office and dictated telegrams.

John and Hazel Head, hosts of the North Gregory Hotel where I had resided for the past two months, turned up a couple of hours after the baby's birth with a double ice-cream cone and a six-pack of XXXX stubbies. I ate the ice-cream and eyed off the beer, wondering what the staff would say. When the sister came in she said, "Lovely! Make sure you have a beer a day, it'll help your milk supply". She was a Middleton girl whose father had at one stage owned the pub of that name. She'd done midwifery in Europe and said it was common practice there to give new breastfeeding mothers beer or stout. I made no objection and the baby thrived.

You would think that having 10 weeks of doing nothing in Winton would have given me enough time to decide on a name, but I was still dithering. I wanted it to be Georgina or Diamantina, both rivers, and decided that, since the Diamantina ran through Kynuna and I'd seen it in flood many

times, that was *the one*. But I registered the name as simply
"Tina". I wish now that I had stuck to my first instinct. I felt it
might go against her in life, but nowadays there are some pretty
unusual names and Diamantina would have fitted in quite well.
After all, Lady Bowen's name was Diamantina.

Barrie eventually got a lift to Winton with a truckie. Travel
by car was still difficult owing to metre-deep ruts on the road
where trucks and cars had been bogged. Unfortunately, having
no wife at hand to cook him a meal, Barrie had eaten a tin
of sardines the night before (his celebratory feast?) and had a
severe attack of the trots, causing the truckie to have to stop
a few times on the track. When it became possible, John Head
drove the three of us back to The Blue Heeler. It was a hairy
ride, with the road still in a bad way, as it often was, in fact
nearly always was.

Tina was a very good baby, perhaps because I didn't have time
to fuss over her! I bought a big old cane pram, secondhand,
from a lady in Winton and it was a godsend. I could wheel
our baby from bedroom to kitchen to bar and always have her
under my eye. In between breastfeeds she often slept in the
pram in our bedroom, which was on the south-west corner of
the pub, near where the trucks pulled in.

The new member of the family was quite a hit with the
customers, especially truckies, and she soon settled in to become
another member of our crew. The customers took the hat
around the day she was born and we started a bank account for
her on the strength of it.

When Tina was about four weeks old, the Kynuna Races
were held, and Barrie was club president. I was so busy I forgot
to feed Tina, but she didn't care; she just slept on. When she
was old enough she spent a fair amount of time in a playpen
in the Ladies' Lounge, lapping up all the attention given to her
by the travellers quenching their thirsts. She had a real bush
christening, baptised by the Rev Michael Hardy on the lawn at
the side of the pub on November 17, 1971, with Christy and
Nellie Black as godparents and Ron and Betty Teece absentee

godparents. Anyone who was around at the time attended this momentous occasion. Even the pub dogs lay around at the foot of the improvised altar for the ceremony. Good old Mad Mick. His lawn came in handy again!

As time went on, Tina had a number of close shaves. On one occasion, a truckie came down the hill after a shower of rain, put on the brakes and skidded several yards into the old spring cart the kids had placed in the front of the pub near the bedroom. They felt it looked like rustic décor. Fortunately only the corner of the veranda was damaged. Tina had a very lucky escape.

On a much later occasion we had a call from the storekeeper to say that Tina had arrived unexpectedly. She'd escaped my attention for a few minutes and walked to the store, a couple of hundred yards away from the pub. The traffic must have been light that day. She covered the distance unscathed.

In time Tina became a Blue Heeler stalwart and helped in all aspects of pubwork, just as the others had.

During my sojourn in Winton a dear soul called Lukie (Lydia), wife of Joe Lucas the carrier/mechanic, came to help out at the pub. She was already a tower of strength to Joe in his business, especially in doing the bookwork and handling of 44-gallon drums of fuel for their trucks.

What a blessing Lukie was. She stayed with us almost to the end of our days at The Heeler and without her having a new baby would have been a nightmare. Tina spent a lot of time with Lukie and gave her that name while she, Tina, was learning to speak. Everyone from then on used that name when referring to one of the West's great women. Mother of eight or nine children of her own.

Lukie was a great cook, and if the mail couldn't get through she would rustle up a batch of bread, damper or scones if necessary, in the blink of an eye, even at times having to sift the weevils out of the flour if it was a bit "old". She also did a great Christmas pud. In fact in every aspect of pub life she coped and often excelled. We served homely type meals, which I think suited the ambience of an outback pub.

One day not long after she had a hip replacement, Lukie was heading off home with a bundle of sheets to wash as our machine had thrown in the towel (pardon the pun). Barrie happened to be riding a horse nearby at the time and offered her a lift. "Hop up behind me, Lukie," he said, and sure enough she rode on the back of the saddle up to her house at the top of the road with her arms full of bedsheets.

We had several excellent girls on our staff at various times before Lukie, and a couple not so good. It was hard to get staff so far from civilisation. One girl we were particularly fond of was Gerri Smith, who got off a bus one day – a Melbourne hairdresser coming to the bush – and stayed for about 10 months, mucking in wherever she was needed – bar, kitchen, laundry or cleaning rooms. A very special lady. She was a great addition to our family.

Life went on with the usual routine of school for the older children. Bob Schwarton, later a Minister in the Queensland Government, was a teacher at one of the small station schools before it closed. He was a humorous and regular customer at our establishment. After their small station school closed, the Mitchell and Howard kids came to Kynuna School. Jesse Mitchell brought them in his "school bus", a Toyota utility with a canopy on the back. In time, Tina would sometimes hitch a ride to school on the bus and save herself a walk.

As we had no kindergarten or pre-school facilities in Kynuna, we felt Tina was missing out on what more closely populated areas could take for granted, and mentioned it to our School Inspector. This resulted in Tina having pre-school by correspondence, with some supervision from the teacher at the time. We were very grateful for this option for Tina who enjoyed it thoroughly. Previously she would sit at the bar or anywhere else around the pub, drawing and "writing". Coincidentally, that School Inspector once taught Barrie at IGS and a different relationship eventuated now that Barrie was an adult. Barrie, in his usual way, greeted the Inspector when he visited with the words, "My Teacher", and threw a few mock punches in his direction.

Joe and "Lukie".

Kynuna State School 1973.

Tina at the school 30 years later.

CHAPTER 18

Surf's Up

A key element of our marketing to tourists was establishing the Kynuna Surf Club. We founded the Club in our first couple of years at the pub, never dreaming it would become well known throughout the world. Overseas travellers who passed our way were anxious to buy some memento of it and told us of sightings of the Surf Club shirt in many of the countries they traversed. Ern once sent us a T-shirt made up by one of the printers at the *QT* with the Surf Club and Barrie featured on it. A very modest effort, however, it gave us the impetus to have shirts professionally printed and we found a man in Ipswich to do the job. He printed shirts for us for many years and they were good sellers. The shirts were white with a mainly blue print, except for the red tongue of a blue cattle dog. Blue Heeler undies were also a good seller with the dog's tongue strategically placed. Our lifesavers' caps were blue and white.

A favourite trick by tourist-coach captains was to get the passengers all primed up to go for a swim when they reached "the Kynuna Surf Club". Some even came into the bar in their swimmers and asked where the water was. Barrie would say, "Oh, the tide's out. You should have been here yesterday". I don't know where they thought the water would come from, hundreds of miles from the coast. Barrie told them, "The tide only comes in with the mail truck".

We proudly took part in the march-past at the annual Winton Outback Festival. We had Tina in Surf Club cap and shirt sitting in a billycart boat. The boys made it with corrugated-iron sides on wheels. We also had a surfboard made from a battered sheet of iron. We marched off with all the "members" in our colours, some pulling the odd-looking cart, with three-year-old Tina in the driving seat. It was quite a sight. We had a lot of fun and also some success as we won the empty beercan-stacking contest and I won the Ladies' Whipcracking contest. My skill at whipcracking learnt in my days on the farm chasing cattle to the different paddocks on dipping days, and yarding up the dairy cattle, came in handy. The things you do for fun out near the droughty Diamantina.

Of course the Club adhered to strict "rules", including banning members from ever calling at a pub that sold hot beer and cold pies and not granting membership to "silvertails". We made an exception for our old mate Bob Katter Junior, as we appreciated his effort for the back country.

We were invited to Government House in Brisbane for a garden party in appreciation of our efforts in raising a great deal of money for the Royal Flying Doctor Service. The resident Governor at the time was Sir James Ramsay and when he shook Barrie's hand he said, "We have something in common you know. You're the Captain of the Kynuna Surf Club and I'm a member of the Nebraska Navy. Well done!!" It was like log cabin to White House for us and we really appreciated it.

I have no doubt it was Barrie's wit that attracted the attention of the *The Sunday Sun* newspaper when they ran a competition in 1972 looking for the Queensland Pub of The Year. Readers were asked to nominate their favourite pub, and give the reason in verse or prose for their choice. There were more entries for our pub than any other. Chris Black, journalist, and photographer, Viv Boland, called in one evening on their tour of the State inspecting the entrants to interview us. (Imagine the job of the newspapermen, visiting half the pubs in

Queensland!) We had a really good night. I don't recall many customers, but we showed them our "wares" and how The Blue Heeler became a popular watering hole, with a Surf Club. We must have met with their approval because we were declared the winner.

Our prize was a handsome wall plaque and the person who wrote the entry – Don Blunt, a bus driver for Skennars – was to receive a year's supply of beer. We'd known Don first as the Culladar mailman and only later as a coach driver. As was the custom for most coach drivers at our establishment he was shouted a softdrink or a cuppa every time he called in, and we had him for morning tea and lunch many a time on Culladar. Unfortunately, Don wasn't happy with his prize – he wanted to swap the beer for cash, he said, to buy a headstone for his late wife's grave. It caused quite a furore at the time. I don't know why, but he blamed us and didn't want to talk to us after that.

Here is Don Blunt's winning entry – a poem:

When you're out Kynuna way
Here's good advice to follow,
Just call at my old favourite pub
It's right there in the hollow.

Patrick will be there to meet you,
He's full of right good cheer
There's redbacks in his rum, I'll swear,
And water in his beer.

He wouldn't take you for a cent,
But watch your bottom dollar.
He sells a sort of pie out there,
His blue dog wouldn't swallow.

I've known him for twenty years,
He has not shouted yet,

The first free one from Barrie
I still have yet to get.

A real character.

Our pub also attracted the attention of television with a few programs filmed at the pub. One featured a pseudo-rescue in the prickly bush gully with the "surf reel". Barrie had to do several takes in the midday sun as he ran back and forth pulling the "reel", which was a roll of barbed wire on a stand with wheels. The on-screen time for that scene was about 20 seconds.

Another show was for the ABC television series *A Big Country*. The story was later included in a publication of stories from the series. The show was called "Journey to Big Rock" and featured a trip to Uluru in a Cobb and Co. tourist coach. Quite a bit of filming was done at the pub. The film crew stayed the night and took in a show, which was written of in the book thus:

> *A hundred pubs from Sydney to Darwin, like The Blue Heeler at Kynuna, offer their bush hospitality to each coachload of tourists that passes through their towns. Kynuna does pretty well out of the passing tourist trade, but the locals provide good value for the travellers in the way of entertainment, too. Everyone enjoys the joke of the existence of a Kynuna Surf Club, the bush music singalong conducted by the publican's wife, and after those long dusty miles, the ice-cold beer.*

The ABC also filmed *A Man's Got to have a Bit of a Go* at the pub. The making of that was hilarious. We tried to buy some of the videos of the relevant shows, but the price was beyond our means, unfortunately. We do, however, have a video of the episode of *This is Your Life* in which Barrie appeared. The star was Beth Garrett, a renowned and revered Flying Doctor pilot and Barrie presented her with a cheque for the RFDS from the Surf Club and The Blue Heeler during the show.

It was quite a trip to make it to that show. Barrie had to catch a plane from Mount Isa and Deb also needed to get back to school in Ipswich, so they set off in the Toyota. It was a very difficult trip, bogging, slipping and sliding from Kynuna to McKinlay, where they arranged for Sid Batt to fly them to The Isa in his light aircraft. This necessitated the use of the bitumen road, the few hundred metres of such pieces of modernity in the centre of McKinlay, as the take-off strip. Barrie left his vehicle there for the return trip. The plane to Brisbane was held up so Barrie and Deb could get on board, still in their muddy clothes, and the Cessna pulled up near the outgoing aircraft to save time. Sid radioed ahead to advise of the delay.

They were booked into the Crest Hotel in Brisbane. On the way up to the room in the lift they were treated like a couple of lepers due to the muddy clothes they were wearing until Barrie announced, "We're rushing to get on *This is Your Life*". The attitude of their fellow lift users changed in an instant.

Incidentally, we experienced a few occasions where "No Room at the Inn" applied until some bystander said to the management, "You must have a room for (1) the Pub of the Year recipient or (2) the publican of The Blue Heeler or (3) the Kynuna Surf Club Captain". A room would suddenly become available.

The equivalent of Tourism Australia invited Barrie to tour Sydney, Melbourne and the Wrest Point Casino in Tasmania with Ted Egan and other entertainers. They put on an outback show for travel agencies from all over the world. Quite an experience. Barrie was always ready to promote the outback, the little township of Kynuna, the Surf Club and of course the Royal Flying Doctor Service.

One year when we were at Noosa on holiday, a letter arrived in Kynuna asking us to attend a function in Brisbane for the presentation of tourism awards, in which the pub was a finalist. The people in charge of the pub at the time omitted to advise us of the fact, and consequently we were taken off the list when we didn't reply to the letter, which we read on our return. I was sorry about that, as it would have been quite an experience, even if we hadn't won.

Pub of the Year trophy.

Kynuna Surf Club Captain.

CHAPTER 19

The Big Wet

Out West you learnt to look at the sky, feel the atmosphere, check the direction of the wind and listen to the occasional weather forecast on Longreach ABC radio. When the wind was a northerly with heavy cloud we knew monsoonal rains, the main seasonal rain out there, were almost certain. The heat becomes almost intolerable with the humidity, as well as the high temperatures, which are the norm in the north-west during the Wet.

Across the road from the pub were the channels of the Diamantina River – across the river was Kynuna Station. The pub was built on the lowest part of the town, which was not good in a big flood. Happily, these didn't occur too often. It was late 1973 and early 1974 when we had our own big Wet, which caused a long and expensive few weeks when we were cut off from the rest of the world.

Many people were caught in town, unable to get to their homes – some for up to six weeks – and they virtually drank the pub dry. We rationed the supplies to so many drinks per person per day by way of a list and finally, practically all we had left in the store room were some bottles of Wild Duck wine and five cartons of old Cairns Draught tallies. Even they didn't last long once they were chilled. Although grog was scarce, people came to the pub daily for the company and entertainment and many a tall tale was told.

Sergeant Pat Tierney came to Kynuna during the floods and was instrumental in getting us an Iroquois helicopter, which proved a godsend for getting food in and stranded people out. Until then, it was every man for himself. No government help or compensation was available. The floodwater came up to the floorboards of the main building and a few inches over the floor in the guest quarters. The longest "holiday" was for a truckie whose semi was bogged in the gully near the pub for nearly three months. That prickly bush gully was where we had engine parts, bread and mail dropped in emergencies. The truckie, Don, checked his truck every day, and found some interesting wildlife taking shelter there. Once a fox took up residence to get away from the water. We in the pub also had a brush with a fox when one raced through the bar, followed closely by a person wielding a mop – me. The fox made his escape out the back door, never to be seen again.

During one wet spell we had the usual full dining room. Our local teacher, Terry, had the misfortune to be seated next to an objectionable drunk who kept falling forward, his hair brushing Terry's dinner when he did so. Our truckie friend, Alan Girdler, was the "waiter" that day. He too was stuck in the Wet and was giving a hand in the dining room, barefooted with tea towel over the shoulder and all. When Terry complained to Alan, he took Terry's meal back to the kitchen and cleaned around the side of the plate with a serviette to make it look presentable. He then took it into the drunken diner and said, "Get this into your guts, you bastard". The objectionable one ate every scrap. What you don't know won't hurt you, they say. Dear Alan, he did us a lot of good turns.

One side-effect of a Wet was a problem with the cash flow. A lot of people travelled through the area with barely enough money to get them to the next town, and of course when it rained and the roads were closed they were practically destitute. In a "state of beggary" as my father might have said. It was difficult to see people unable to afford to eat and we tried to help some of them with a feed for a job, but we were never in the financial position to give too many handouts. One way we could help was to make sure the post office had a supply of cash. It was also a Commonwealth Bank agency and we deposited our cash takings in our account there daily to give the postmaster (or mistress) a cash flow to at least cater for those people who had Commonwealth Bank accounts or money wired to them from their friends or relations.

After a few weeks and the roads became passable, we needed the money in our business account to pay our bills. We took it out of our personal post office account in cheque form to pay into our business account at the Bank of New South Wales (as it was known then) in Winton. The Commonwealth Bank didn't like that, accusing us of making a convenience of them and they asked us to desist. The person in charge of the post office was getting paid a percentage on deposits and withdrawals to operate the bank agency and it was apparently costing the bank too much. It got our danders up! How lousy! We closed the Commonwealth Bank account and never banked with them again. We even closed the kids' school bankbook accounts. We later opened a Bank of New South Wales agency in the pub, which effectively solved the cash-flow problem for travellers and locals.

During the big flood of early 1974, our boys were in danger of missing the start of high school, where they were to stay with Ern and Eva to attend Ipswich State High. It was Duncan's first year and Steven's third. The Army Iroquois helicopter did a few flights out of town and took some travellers and all the high school children to Julia Creek. From there our boys flew to Townsville by Fokker Friendship, then to Brisbane by a Boeing 727. Brisbane and Ipswich too were in flood, and the trip from the Brisbane Airport to Brassall took three hours through flood-delayed traffic. We were very relieved that our boys arrived in time for school, but I don't suppose they were all that thrilled. The school itself was damaged by the flood and the start to the school year was delayed. A massive clean-up was required before the school term could begin on February 11. The boys had their photo in the *QT* as they chatted to the headmaster, Frank Underwood, about their epic journey.

Then came Cyclone Tracy at the end of 1974. This tropical cyclone devastated the city of Darwin in the Northern Territory from Christmas Eve to Christmas Day, 1974. We were lying in bed on Christmas morning at the end of 1974 listening to the news about Cyclone Tracy on the radio. Tina was in with us playing with a new crying doll that Santa had brought her. We kept hearing noises, which we put down to the new doll, but after a while realised it wasn't the doll at all. We looked under the bed, and there was Leggy having a litter of pups. Some had already been born while we were sleeping.

Deb kept Leggy under surveillance for the rest of the day. She ran out to us in the bar, blood on her face, and sang out, "Another one's just come out". What an education for her and what a picture. As traffic headed south fleeing the awful devastation in Darwin we became very busy.

In 1976, we were hit by Cyclone Ted. A pilot in McKinlay phoned and told us of the wind-speed his aircraft had registered so we knew we were in for a rough time. Barrie was worried about the lifting roof on the front veranda. While everyone was sensibly taking shelter, we went out into the storm and with great effort roped down the roof beams, barely able to keep on our feet. The sandblasting on our legs from the dirt frontage was painful and when the job was done we were pleased to retreat to the safety of the bar. Our poor old galah in his cage on the front veranda went for a rocky ride, being blown quite a distance. He died, probably of shock, a few days later. The cattle stood up against the fences with their backs to the wind, but couldn't escape the fury of the cyclone. It caused a lot of damage around Kynuna and left many dead cattle in its wake.

Hanging in the bar in a prominent position was what we called a Snake Charmer, a long length of heavy thick wire, twisted and fashioned with a handle to be used in case a snake needed dispatching. I recall it being used a couple of times.

Once I put my hand on a snake in a cupboard containing wine bottles. Fortunately it turned out to be a child python and not venomous.

One year when the Diamantina was in flood, I was outside rolling up a large extension cord. Unbeknown to me, a Downs tiger snake was tangled up in the cord and started flapping around my legs in a frenzy. It must have been startled, but no more than I was. I started to scream for help – probably the worst thing I could have done, as it stirred the snake into more activity. Anyway, it eventually took off at speed, and I went inside in a state of shock.

I demanded to know why no-one sitting around the bar came to my aid. They said they didn't hear me. They had a Slim Dusty tape going full blast. I had a sore throat for a day or two from my yelling, but that was a cheap price to pay for surviving my encounter with the Joe Blake. It was fortunate I didn't get bitten as the only way I could have been evacuated was by air, and the bitumen street was the only place an aircraft could land. The Diamantina was in flood and we were cut off from civilisation in all directions. Helicopters were more rare in those days and very expensive to hire, although I suppose the expense could have been justified if it meant saving my life. We didn't have any service like Air Ambulance or Care Flight with their helicopters to call on in those days.

One year we had the most awful rat plague. They chewed everything they could get their teeth into. Our boys had heaps of fun killing them with their air rifles. They lined them up as they came around the door of the bar and let them have it. Our old blue bitch, Leggie, was a keen rat hunter. Every morning we found a great heap of dead rats she had piled up on the lawn.

Rats weren't the only cursed pests. The gidgee bugs nearly drove a person mad when they invaded the district, usually after a Wet season. Their smell and taste – if you accidentally got one in your mouth – was atrocious. We turned the lights off at night and used kerosene lights, candle power or carbide lights to try to deter the bugs. They were into everything: hair, dinner, clothes and most distressingly, your beer! The morning after, when they were at their most rampant, we swept up about half a 44-gallon drum of the little beasties from within the building.

Although flooding was dreaded, the kids loved a good shower of rain or a storm, because they often didn't see rain for months on end. They used a beer carton, or anything else they could lay their hands on, to slide about in the gutters, revelling in the unusual event of something falling out of the sky. They ended up nice and muddy, but it was worth it to see the joy they received from the sky's gift. Sometimes they even found little fish that sailed down the gutters, another gift from above. Once during a good stretch of rain when the CWA hall was full of stranded travellers, some Asian people caught and cooked the little fish. I bet they were bony. I still don't know where those little fish came from. The kids were so used to living in the dry West that once when visiting the Patricks in Ipswich the little ones wondered why the grass in the back yard was wet. Night dew was an unknown novelty.

During an extended wet-weather period when for a change we weren't inundated with stranded "guests", I used drums of white paint we had on hand to paint the pub when the rain stopped. I went "up the ladder" first thing in the morning and worked on it until day's end. The kids and a couple of their mates were at home on school holidays at the time and with the aid of our staff, kept themselves "fed and watered" for the day. Duncan became very good at cooking a few of his favourite snacks, including puftaloons and cheesecakes, and had to fight the others off his delicacies, ending up doing only half the amount, ensuring insufficient to feed the rest of the mob. It encouraged them to have a go themselves. The painting eventually was finished – white with turquoise trim. The outer walls were corrugated iron and a paint roller fitting the "corrugates" made things a little easier.

Dust storms were also dreaded. Although we closed everything if we saw one coming, it was still a mammoth job getting rid of the dust left behind. It'd get into every nook and cranny and there were a lot of those in the old building. If it

rained straight after such an event, everything turned to mud.
The joys of outback living.

The boys discussing the flood evacuation with their principal.

CHAPTER 20

Who Wants to be a Millionaire?

While we were doing all right in the pub, we were always on the lookout for anything that might improve business, as you do. At one stage there was a big announcement: Shale Oil In Julia Creek! This aroused our interest and we could see dollars coming from the increased traffic a mine would create. The paper reported: *It is considered almost certain that Julia Creek will get a shale-oil project worth $100 million.* Joh Bjelke-Petersen was the Premier of Queensland. Alas, nothing happened.

We always hoped for a big upgrade of the highway, with the expectation of an increase in business with the presence of road gangs and other workers. When Bill Glasson, who was the Member for Gregory from 1974 to 1989, remarked in 1975 that if the Landsborough Highway was sealed within the next 15 years he'd "walk to Bourke with a waterbag" (better than without one I suppose), I sent robust Letters to the Editors of the newspapers in Brisbane. At the time, Bill Glasson was pressing for the Boulia to Winton road to be sealed and we felt he was biased against the Landsborough Highway. As it turned out, the work on the highway began in 1980, just after we sold the pub.

In 1977 there was a wealthy man from Brazil trying to buy up Queensland properties and it was rumoured that he might want the pub. Barrie and I had many discussions about the pros and cons. Should we grab the money and run, or hold on? We felt that selling to a Brazilian would be most unAustralian, even though the thought was tempting. In the end we decided to remain patriotic and keep The Blue Heeler in Aussie hands. Barrie was a particularly patriotic Aussie. However, we were never put to the test.

Even though we were happy in Kynuna and had a lot of friends in the district and among the travelling public, the thought of retiring to the coast was very tempting, and if someone offered enough money we would have accepted. Occasionally phony buyers came along. One pair rang from Winton to say they definitely wanted the pub because they'd already looked it over (unbeknown to us). They were keen to make a good offer and would arrive about breakfast time. I cooked them a good breakfast and they had a couple of drinks. As a gesture of goodwill we didn't charge them. They said their solicitor would be in touch that day and took off for The Curry. We never heard from them again, but it was a good lesson to be on the alert for fraudsters. Sometimes dreams overtake reality and common sense. These two were people we had previously known and thought were honest. You live and learn.

At one stage we took on an agency for batteries and tyres. There was no service station from Winton to Cloncurry and the road was very hard on tyres. Our old friend Joe Lucas helped motorists out at times, changing their tyres and doing odd jobs on their cars, having had plenty of experience with his own vehicles during his many years as a carrier in the district. At the time of our going into this extra service, we put up lights along the front veranda and signage supplied by the tyre and battery people, which caused some angst among a few locals.

Joe with his knowledge of things mechanical was a great asset to the district, especially after he retired. He helped us out at the pub on numerous occasions and was equally generous with the travelling public. He was very versatile, able to usually get a driver in trouble on to the next stop where more serious repairs could be made. A true bush mechanic. Joe was an old style bushie. To advertise his presence at the back door of the kitchen, he'd yell out, "Something burning?" He was also fond of saying, "Send her down, Hughie" whenever it started to rain. The West was littered with humorous old-timers.

One of my few regrets concerns the day we had a call from an art dealer in Brisbane. He offered us first option on a painting of the hotel by Hugh Sawrey, the iconic Australian artist. Sawrey had visited the pub while we were away on holidays and painted it, fighting cattle dogs and all. We were sorry we'd missed him. I happened to be going to Brisbane at the time so called in to view it. It was a good opportunity, but a bit beyond our resources, so we regretfully declined. Someone we knew bought it and later sold it at a great profit. Sawrey left a couple of his rough sketches for the publican and at least we ended up with those.

Another time we lived to rue the day was when we decided to bank all the 50-cent coins we'd let accumulate in our safe. I took the loot into the bank in Winton. I could hardly carry the bucket of coins inside, so heavy were they. I'm glad bushrangers weren't around in those days. It wasn't long after this that some travellers asked if they could buy all our 50-cent coins. They offered up to $3 a coin. I nearly cried at the thought. The coins in those days contained a lot of silver and were quite sought after, especially from silly bushies like us!

Having a business in Kynuna meant being on all the committees, participating in all social functions, donating to every fund going, selling raffle tickets and donating prizes. We were on the school and race club committees, where Barrie was president of both at various times over the years. I had a short stint as an office-bearer on the CWA and was always on the school committee. I was treasurer of the Rodeo and Sporting

Association for about nine years and worked very well with the secretary, John Markwell. We were very proud of our efforts in raising money for the Queensland section of the Royal Flying Doctor Service at our annual rodeo, Bushman's Carnival or gymkhana. I decided to quit that position when a meeting stacked by people who never normally attended meetings altered the workings of the association, with new office-bearers appointed. To add insult to injury, one local "lady" stubbed her cigarettes out on the floor of our dining room where the meeting was held, leaving her mark on our newly laid vinyl. Have you never heard of ashtrays, Madam? Nearly everyone smoked in those days.

What annoyed us more was the distribution of the funds raised at the next rodeo. Instead of being donated to the RFDS that year nearly all the profits raised went to purchasing portable yards. The old wooden yards weren't considered good enough. The new portable (steel) yards could be moved to other situations, particularly office-bearers' properties, if required. I believe the committee men, all cattle owners, had more use out of the new facility than the Association, which only used the yards for a couple of days of the year. The RFDS operated 24 hours a day, 365 days a year and served more than just a few station owners.

At events run by the Rodeo and Sporting Association I competed in bending, flag and barrel races, and one year even made an unsuccessful attempt at camp drafting. I had never drafted and didn't even get the beast out of the yard. How embarrassing! But it was in the spirit of having-a-go and the more entries there were, the more money was raised. I usually borrowed a horse to compete, as we only owned a horse for a short period. There were gymkhanas held at the racecourse at one stage and I participated in any event I could: foot races, tug-of-wars and even ladies woodchopping, as well as in the horse events – the straight gallop included. There was also an event called The Paddy Melon Race. The melons were collected beforehand from the downs, where they grew wild. I was always enthusiastic, but never won too many events. In between being treasurer, raffle-ticket seller, contestant and publican, it was a busy day. Cricket matches too were held occasionally on the claypan not far from the pub. The dress of the players varied from cricket whites to ringer's attire of hats, boots and all.

It was certainly a life of hard work. I could lift two cartons of stubbies at once, usually when unloading a few tons of beer off a semi. If by chance I had the opportunity for a sit-down in the pub – while minding the bar during a lull in business, I became addicted to *The Australasian Post,* to which we subscribed. This was about all the reading matter we had time for, except for *The North Queensland Register,* which came weekly. The other magazine we liked was *People* with cartoon strips by McClure. When a cartoon appeared that resonated with our way of life we cut it out and pasted it on a wall. However, it was the crosswords that got me in, and I worked on them when possible with the help of a passing truckie, if he was so inclined. I still have a passion for crosswords, but nowadays am making up for the lack of time to read during all those years out West, and one of the first things I did upon leaving the Back Country was to order a daily paper delivery.

I suppose we were lucky, health wise, in that more trips to the hospital weren't required over our 14 years in Kynuna, although when Barrie was on tour in Tasmania with Ted Egan, I badly damaged my left ankle. I was getting over a fence to feed the pigs with a bucket of food scraps in hand. A local drove me to the hospital in Julia Creek. This put me in a pretty tricky position, running the pub with a leg in plaster and using crutches, while Barrie was entertaining "the masses" in the south. I managed somehow.

On another occasion Barrie was helping unload a cargo of beer from a semi-trailer bogged on the road to McKinlay when he injured his hand. He jumped off the trailer, with his hand on a "gate" with very roughly welded edges and ended up with large, deep gashes on his fingers. He came back to the pub and stood under the shower. In the process, he lost a lot of blood which he neglected to mention to anyone. By next morning he couldn't get off the bed. A local put him on a mattress in the back of our Holden wagon and took him to Julia Creek. He had almost bled to death. I drove Barrie to Julia Creek once when he couldn't swallow – not even saliva. A needle at the hospital soon had him OK but it was the first diagnosis of his Globus Hystericus (a swallowing disorder now called Globus Pharnyngeus). This trying condition would plague him for the rest of his life.

Bull, our faithful blue dog and the inspiration of our business name, left his station behind the bar on April 15, 1975. It was a sad time for us when the mascot of the pub eventually became too incapacitated to keep going. Barrie had to put Bull down and that night wrote to the boys who were away at school. *I shot Old Bull tonight*, he began. Bull had served many years as custodian behind the bar. His place was taken by Bull 2.

In 1979 a gang arrived, booked into the pub and started work on the powerlines to connect Kynuna to the mains power coming from Julia Creek. It was a very exciting and busy time for us. The thought of getting rid of the old motors put a spring in our step, and it was a chance to make a bit of money through the extra trade with all our new boarders. We needed the extra income to buy the new appliances we would need, too.

We made large amounts of sandwiches every day for the men to take out on the job, and with the extra people for all meals, and the cleaning of rooms, we had little time to spare. We also had an electrician on site to rewire the premises ready for the switchover.

It was during this time that we lost our little Australian terrier, Tammy. The power gang, mostly from Kingaroy, the peanut capital of Australia, went home for some R & R and returned bearing lots of boiled salted peanuts. At night they sat in their rooms, playing cards and eating salted peanuts, putting their shells into used ice-cream containers on the floor. Tammy found the salted shells tempting, ate too many and fell sick. Too much salt, apparently. Barrie had no trouble diagnosing the problem with his knowledge of animal husbandry learnt from his Stock Inspector study and experience. She was in awful agony and Barrie decided she had to be put down. A local came, picked her up and took her out bush and shot her. It was the kindest thing to do, but it was a very sad day.

We had a great old celebration when the power was switched on. It made life a lot easier for us in the pub, no longer pumping diesel from 44-gallon drums to fuel up the motors, and it relieved us of the worry of break-downs. And of course no longer the heavy job of getting the diesels started, with their big flywheels, a job that I often had to do if Barrie was not on the scene. Storms and other interruptions still occurred, but now it was up to someone else to fix those problems. Power was very expensive out West, something we noticed when we went to live in Julia Creek where we paid double what it cost us in Toowoomba. I can't remember what it was in Kynuna after we were connected to the grid, but the expense was worth it.

Our kids said they missed the beat of the old motors to help put them to sleep at bedtime. I can't say I felt the same. It was just the lifting of a great burden for me.

After a few years of constant work, we started to take annual holidays in Noosa, which were always eagerly anticipated. We relied on some very staunch and capable friends to hold the fort while we had a break, for which we were most grateful. Our children attended the Tewantin School during these sojourns and after school would get off the school bus, drop their schoolbags and get into the putt-putt with us to go tailor fishing on the North Shore beach. I had some "smoko" for them in the boat, usually cream buns, a much sought-after treat only available while on holidays.

We were at Noosa on holiday when "Man landed on the Moon". We came in early from fishing to watch it on TV. The kids were very young and I don't think it meant as much to them.

We sometimes camped on Teewah Beach with the kids during our holidays, often driving there in our friend Lloyd

Dwyer's old Volkswagen Kombi, a floral décor painted old beach buggy called "SpitsandFartz". That is about how it went too. Once, stranded by a combination of sandmining and a high tide, we spent hours sitting in the rain under a tarp in the back of the vehicle waiting for the tide to go out. We camped in two-man tents, an old derelict bus or an old hut that was eventually demolished. "Up the beach" was a favourite part of the holidays.

At the end of the holiday we filled up a large Esky with ice, salt and fish to take back to Kynuna with us. If we hadn't caught enough, we'd buy mullet from local fishermen. Fish out West was a welcome addition to the pub menu.

One year Barrie, in need of a bit of early R & R, decided to go for a holiday on his own. He booked into an island resort on South Mole and set off, armed with a lovely big new beach towel, to be a beach-bum for a while. Some coot stole his new towel so he packed up and went to Townsville and spent the rest of the holiday with his mate, Les Llewellyn, who owned a hotel there. More his style.

In 1976 my delightful mother-in-law, Eva, as elegant as ever at 65, decided to come to Kynuna for Christmas. Father stayed at home, feeling that the bus trip would be too much for him. No sooner had she walked into The Heeler than we got a phone message from Ipswich to say that Ern was in hospital and not expected to live.

Barrie took off in the car for Ipswich with Eva. They arrived home before Ern died on December 26, 1976.

The clergy who spoke at Ern's funeral paid tribute to his long service to sport and journalism and his unfailing championing of the causes of Ipswich and district. Ern was on the editorial staff of the *Queensland Times* for more than 40 years, nine spent as editor, and had lectured in journalism at the Queensland University.

In the mid-1940s, Ern introduced the Sportographs column to the *QT*. He became an authority on local sport, passing on his knowledge through print and radio. His opinions were eagerly sought by members of the Queensland Rugby League. Ern was the manager of the Queensland team, a highlight of which was the team's 1951 success in Sydney. Ern was President of the Ipswich Rugby League for a time also.

Kids with fish during a Noosa holiday at 'Waldor'.

Tina at Noosaville.

CHAPTER 21

Our Worst Nightmare

As the oldest, Steven left home first. After Grade 10 he began his apprenticeship as a mechanical fitter with Queensland Railways in Townsville in North Queensland. Our good friend King Glendon found him a place to board and helped him through the first few weeks (as he did for Duncan when he also did his fitter's apprenticeship in Townsville).

Steven later transferred to the Ipswich Railway Workshops a couple of years after his grandfather died. He said he wanted to live with Grandma Eva and be of some help to her. Deb was also living there in the Patrick family home. After completing his apprenticeship in 1979, Steven moved to Mount Isa and worked for Mount Isa Mines. We were expecting him at Kynuna for Christmas and we were most disappointed when he couldn't come – he'd succumbed to a bad case of mumps and spent Christmas in Mount Isa Hospital. A Salvation Army officer gave him a toiletry pack, the only gift he received.

We would never see him again.

We were working in the bar one night in March when we received a phone call from Barrie's brother, Don, who was living and working in Mount Isa at the time. He had the dreadful job of telling us his nephew and our firstborn son, Steven, had been killed and he had just been to identify him. They each in their own way must have been easy to connect in a town the size of Mount Isa.

It was the most devastating news. Steven was riding his motorbike to visit a friend in the hospital at about 4pm when a drunk driver failed to see a stop sign and hit him at a street intersection. He suffered a ruptured aorta and bled to death at the scene. It was March 21, 1980. He was just 20 years old.

Steve was buried in the Mount Isa Cemetery with a large contingent of members of the Desert Rats Motor Cycle Club acting as pallbearers, then leading the procession to the cemetery, green traffic lights all the way. Church of England Minister Ray Ayles, a man we knew well, conducted the funeral service. At Barrie's request a piper from the Mount Isa Pipe Band played "Amazing Grace". In our shows for the tourists, that song had always been one of Barrie's favourites. Listening to the plaintive tones of the piper made for an intensely moving experience. We sent a cheque to the Pipe Band for the piper, but it was returned. They don't charge, they said.

Eva, who couldn't make it to Mount Isa, sat on the polished timber toolbox that belonged to Steve in his old bedroom in Ipswich and cried as the sad event took place in faraway Mount Isa. The Kynuna-ites who attended escorted our vehicle back to The Heeler. We appreciated their company on the road and the kind thoughts of our neighbours.

To lose a parent or a spouse is distressing, but to lose a child is devastating. Steven was a lovely person – kind and gentle in a certain way and I think he had the Patrick "music gene", although he never made the most of that ability. He also loved motorbikes and was in the middle of restoring an old Triumph Bonneville, making one bike out of two old ones. His motorcycling mates in Mount Isa vowed they'd finish the job.

The motorist who caused the accident received a very light punishment, or should that be "sentence", for his part in this life-changing event in our lives.

Barrie and I went on after the funeral – the first I'd ever attended strangely enough – and kept working hard. We never did a lot of open mourning. I think we kind of kept things bottled up, each afraid of upsetting the other, but if one was down, the other coped until the equilibrium was restored and vice versa. We worked as a silent team, each always aware of the pain of the other. Whenever we heard the song "Amazing Grace" – then and throughout our lives in the future – it was utterly heart wrenching.

Just prior to Steven's death, Jack and Pam May were urging us to sell them the pub. The very day that Reverend Ayles came to discuss the funeral, Pam happened to ring and said they were getting impatient.

Barrie said, "I'm arranging my son's funeral, ring me in a few weeks". Jack and Pam didn't know about Steven's death and probably felt bad about phoning at such a time.

A couple of weeks later Pam rang again and Barrie told her we'd made a decision. We wanted "out". We were slaving in the West, rarely seeing our children, and after losing Steve, we lost heart. They could have The Blue Heeler.

And so on May 29, 1980, we drove out of Kynuna, on to our new life in south-east Queensland. With the construction of the Landsborough Highway to bitumen standard due in the next few years, we nevertheless left before the business would reach its peak. Selling then would make the price we got for the pub look like "small beer", but regardless of monetary aspects, we were keen to get out and they were pleased to take over. Good luck to them! I wonder if the travellers missed our little shows.

As fate would have it, I also lost my dear old Dad during this time and it was with great sadness that I missed his funeral on the day we left the pub. He was the best dad a girl could hope for and I still reflect on his teachings to help me through life.

The trauma of losing Steve continued for a considerable length of time. After settling back in the south-east at Noosaville, in a unit we had bought on Gympie Terrace about a year before, my frame of mind worsened. I found myself going over and over Steve's death, talking to myself in anger and feeling much hatred towards the motorist, but unable to talk about it to Barrie in case it exacerbated his low state of mind. We were still skirting around the subject, each afraid of upsetting the other. In hindsight, we should have discussed it more and let go of our feelings, instead of being so stoic. Eventually I consulted our much-valued medico in Noosaville, Dr Kahl. He said that I would have to let go and try to get the hatred out of my heart and look to the future. Nothing would change by mulling over it except my health, which would deteriorate, mentally and physically. Anger against the man wouldn't help. He gave me some pills and, along with his good advice, they got me on the road to normality once more.

Steven was a kind and gentle soul.

Chapter 22

Sea Change

Every time we left the pub for a break we went to Noosa, our favourite holiday destination. We were always warmly greeted by the locals and Barrie was somewhat of a celebrity, especially around Tewantin and was known as "The Heeler". While on holidays photos of us dining out often appeared in the local paper; now we were locals, part of the mob.

One of the first things Barrie wanted (needed?) was a boat of his own. So, after hiring "O" Boats from Len Ely all Barrie's fishing life, we became the proud owners of a yellow and white 14'6" Haines Hunter half-cabin cruiser. What fun and satisfaction we derived from her over the next few years. Barrie spent hours sharpening his filleting knives, stretching the lines and making sure the fishing gear was ready to go. We'd "go prawning" at night to gather bait, dragging the prawn net, up to the armpits in water in the river and creeks. If they were big enough, we ate the prawns we netted. A few years later when the Haines was getting a bit heavy for us to handle, we exchanged it for a "tinnie". This smaller boat allowed us to go into more shallow water, chasing the elusive crab.

After we settled at Noosaville, we thought it wise to invest in more real estate. After passing up many deals, which in hindsight would have made us rich, we settled on a modest, new, three-bedroom brick home in Niblick Street, Noosa River Heights (we kept our unit on Gympie Terrace). From our new home Tina attended the Tewantin State School. Tina said she was the only kid in her class with "old" parents and ones that weren't divorced. A slight exaggeration, but a different world, Noosa, compared to the West. While we were living there Tina broke her arm playing in the park with the local children. Six weeks later while roller-skating, she broke the same arm again. She enjoyed the extracurricular benefits of living in a more populated part of Australia, but was encountering a few hazards along the way! Deb was by this time happily married to her husband, Graeme Harding, and Duncan was forging his career as a fixed-wing and helicopter pilot.

We'd left all our furniture and goods and chattels behind in Kynuna and had to completely outfit the house, from cutlery to washing machine and everything in between. We did bring some framed pictures and memorabilia with us and finally unpacked a number of wedding presents that we'd toted around Queensland for 25 years.

After taking it easy for a while, Barrie got a job as evening doorman at the Royal Mail Hotel in Tewantin and I started as barmaid in the public bar. I think at that stage that the Reef Hotel was the only other pub in Noosa. The Villa Noosa Hotel at Noosaville opened not long after. I worked from 11am to 3pm Monday to Friday, which suited Tina's school hours. The public bar of the Royal Mail was extremely busy in the hours I worked. In the '40s and '50s the Mail had been especially popular with honeymooners as it was considered quite "posh". It was still a well-run and popular establishment when Barrie and I joined it and Merv Lee was the boss. He treated us very well. Many of our friends were regulars. One April, Barrie brought a tiny little dog into the bar – my birthday present! We called her Happy.

Fishing continued to be an important part of our lives. In those days the fishing was still good, although nothing like it had been back in the '50s. Tina settled in and became involved in different pursuits such as ballet and guitar lessons, both unattainable in the West. Netball became her passion and she played for a team at Tewantin and later went to New Zealand with a school team.

I usually took Tina to netball on Saturday afternoons and on one such day we nearly had a catastrophe in the house. Barrie was at home watching the rugby league on TV (one of the great pleasures of coastal life). When he got a bit peckish, he decided to fry some chips. When Tina and I got home the house was full of smoke – Barrie had concentrated too much on the football instead of his cooking and ended up with a fat fire. Putting the frying pan in the sink was a bad idea, as it caused the roller blind to catch fire. When endeavouring to put out the fire in the blind, his much treasured leather jacket caught fire, but luckily he shed it smartly. The final result was a house interior that had to be repainted, the smoky walls reminiscent of The Blue Heeler kitchen when we bought it. Luckily, insurance covered the costs of the kitchen repairs and a new leather jacket.

On another occasion, Barrie accidentally backed the Toyota Land Cruiser wagon into the Noosa River. He was going to check crab-pots and was backing the boat in. But owing to a strong outgoing tide and a strong "fresh" in the river, the brakes didn't do their duty and the whole lot ended up in the river. Barrie got out just before the vehicle was completely submerged. All you could see was the floating boat, and the aerial of the wagon showing above water. Vehicle and boat were towed out and Barrie arrived home very cold and down-hearted. A wet tail and no fish! The car had to be extensively dried out and checked over, and was devalued when it came to trading it in later. The amazing thing is that Barrie was a very careful, risk-averse person, which proves that accidents can happen to the best of us.

We had been back living in south-east Queensland for just over a year when my dear mother left us. She died of cancer on July 7, 1981 three weeks after being diagnosed. Mum's departure left a great hole in the lives of her children. She is remembered as a strong, resourceful lady who faced many hard times and dry gullies on her journey through life. She brought up eight children, all of whom led successful and productive lives.

The Tewantin RSL asked Barrie to start up a club bar in their premises. He agreed and we rented a "hut" up on the Noosa North Shore for a week and put our heads together, making lists of requirements for a new club. We had to start from scratch. Everything from bar mats, glasses, drinks, chips, peanuts, kegs and fittings had to be ordered. It was quite an undertaking but a task we enjoyed. The grand opening was on September 14, 1981. Barrie was manager and I was part-time barmaid.

Barrie considered Gae Hocking the best barmaid for miles around and hired her to work in the bar. Barrie and I did quite a bit of entertaining along the lines of The Blue Heeler – toned down a little! – and the piano and piano-accordion came in for plenty of use.

After a year or two at the Tewantin RSL, Barrie decided to return to stock work and applied to the Department of Primary Industry (DPI) to be re-employed. He was successful and did a few months in Brisbane mainly dealing with the racing industry. Barrie would always do well in his promotion exams in the DPI. He had a phenomenal memory, which was an asset during his studies, and was always near the top of the class if not top.

His work base was the Brisbane Stock Office at the Animal Research Institute, Yeerongpilly on Brisbane's westside. For four nights a week he stayed with Deb and Graeme at their property in Karralee, outside Ipswich, returning to Tewantin at weekends. He often had weekend jobs in the Sunshine Coast district and at times I went with him. I especially remember horse sales at Eumundi, where I helped him with bookwork.

During his first stint with the DPI, Barrie had his eye on a posting to Toogoolawah, once a dairying region north of Ipswich. Instead he was sent to Toowoomba then Julia Creek. This time his luck was in. Early in 1985 (with Barrie now a little over 50), we moved to Toogoolawah and took up residence in a "department house". We were very happy with this posting and found Toogoolawah a most friendly town. On driving around in our new and noticeable yellow Toyota Hi-Lux we found that nearly every motorist gave the "finger-off-the-steering wheel" wave. We discovered many citizens in the district were of the Apostolic Religion, no doubt going back to the early German settlers. They made for a very strong community.

Barrie at different times specialised in Deer Farming and Feed Lot operations, which kept him pretty busy and away from home on occasion, with "The Wifey" still taking phone calls at home at all hours. But the life of a Stock Inspector in a small country town has much to commend it and Barrie enjoyed his posting. He had a bit of fun with a couple of the local "cockies", even if they didn't know it. If they phoned him with "Featherstonehaugh here" or similar in a high-falutin' voice, Barrie would retort with an equally haughty "Patrick here". The landed gentry!

Barrie was later given one of the newest positions in the Queensland Public Service, that of Feedlot Services Group Specialist Licensing Inspector for the Brisbane Valley and Burnett regions. Vern Doyle took over the normal Stock Inspector's duties, but we stayed on in the departmental residence.

In March 1990, I went on a trip to Ha Hei in New Zealand with my sister, Ann, for a Harsant Family Reunion. It was also attended by other members of the "Australian Harsants". We hired a car for the first week, driving round the North Island, then caught the ferry from Wellington to the South Island where we toured by coach for a week. Before leaving Toogoolawah I froze enough dinners for Barrie for the duration to make sure he ate properly while I was away. Toogoolawah was a pretty busy Stock office and I thought if he came in very tired at night it would be very easy for him to microwave "a feed" as Barrie called it.

However, on the first night I was away Barrie must have been drowning his sorrows at his favourite local "watering hole" (missing me already) because when he took his meal out of the oven he discovered that he'd heated up a container of frozen mango by mistake. He gave up in disgust and went to bed without dinner. A local chap had given me a box of beautiful home-grown mangoes and in my usual economical "waste-not, want-not" mode, I'd frozen the flesh in containers for future fruit salads when the mango season was over. I think Barrie was glad to see me upon my return. (Even if only for my cooking.)

Tina attended high school in Toogoolawah. It was only a high school top and students in Years 11 and 12 had to go by bus to the larger Kilcoy High School, so we decided to enrol her at the Ipswich Girls' Grammar School (IGGS), my old school, as a boarder. Of course the way things go, Murphy's Law and all that, by the time Tina was ready to go into Year 11, Toogoolawah had expanded into a high school that catered for senior students. But we decided the experience of boarding away from the small town of Toogoolawah and meeting new people would be worthwhile. I don't think the experience was as fulfilling for her as it was for me, but of course she had gained a lot more of life's experiences by that stage, whereas I had known little beyond the confines of the Radford-Harrisville district. For me it had been very exciting to leave the nest of the Harsant farm.

Tina learnt to drive on the trips to and from IGGS. You didn't need a logbook or learner's permit in those days. Whether I was a good teacher or not is a matter for conjecture, but I think she became a proficient driver.

Not too long after we moved to Toogoolawah, I started working part-time at the Toogoolawah Post Office. I enjoyed the work and spent about nine years there, retiring in 1995 at 60 years of age. Computers were just coming into general usage in the post office and I regret that I missed out on the chance to get computer savvy, but Barrie's health was deteriorating and he required more of my time.

In November 1993 Barrie was diagnosed with emphysema and he resigned from the DPI. We had already bought a block of land in Annette Street, a lovely spot overlooking the golf course, and built a house there to Barrie's design, which we enjoyed living in.

When Barrie turned 60 the following year, the family gave him a birthday party at Deb and Graeme's home. It was a huge surprise – I got him there by fair means or foul – and he was absolutely amazed to see the guests who had gathered from far and wide in his honour. Old friends – stockies, cockies, truckies, schoolies, rellies, the lot. He wasn't feeling all that well, but managed to have a good afternoon, and to see such a wide range of friends, some of whom we hadn't seen for years, made for a great afternoon of reminiscing.

Deb and Graeme suggested we sell the Annette Street house and move to their 26-acre block in Karrabin, as the council gave approval for a "family subdivision" on which we could build. So we got an acre of ground from them and once again built a house. We chose almost the same design as the Toogoolawah house with a couple of enlargements and moved in during January 1998. When Happy died, we decided to no longer have a dog, and installed a security system instead. We still hoped to spend a lot of time at Noosaville and were thinking of the kennel charges we would save.

Some people said we were making a big mistake being so close to family as we would end up being unpaid babysitters. They could not have been more wrong, as we got nothing but pleasure from our grandchildren, Harry and Bronte, and for quite a while had them for dinner every Wednesday night, often picking them up after school. They always called us Bazza and Grandma. They were, and still are, a delight.

Living on the outskirts of the fast-growing City of Ipswich had all the benefits of being near medical assistance – doctor, hospital and ambulance – and being only 15 minutes from town. It is a wonderful place to live with plenty of kangaroos, wallabies, hares and every sort of bird, especially butcherbirds, and yes, crows. Apart from the birds, the only other noise is an occasional jet from Amberley Air Base. Thank God we have them. The jets, I mean.

Unfortunately Barrie did not have long in this little heavenly corner of the world as his health quickly deteriorated. He also developed a pre-malignant skin condition called Mycosis-Fungoides and for many months I took him weekly, or sometimes more often, to Toowong in Brisbane for treatment. In the end the travelling became too wearing, so he stopped the treatment saying it was killing him quicker than the disease. He was eventually admitted to St Andrew's Hospital in Ipswich with severe chronic obstructive pulmonary disease and died a few days later in his 69th year. It was just over 20 years since his mother passed away. Eva had died on November 1, 1982 at 72 years of age and Barrie died on November 6, 2002.

Barrie's funeral service and cremation took place on Armistice Day at 11am on the 11th of November, being preceded by the traditional Armistice Day's minute's silence. It was fitting, as Barrie was one of the most patriotic of Australians, having great regard for those who served this country in war and peace. With this in mind, I placed an Australian flag on his coffin.

We later scattered Barrie's ashes in the Noosa River from a boat. Duncan took Barrie's favourite fishing rod with him, and as we scattered the ashes and some roses, Duncan got a bite, and landed a nice fish at the right moment to commemorate the occasion. We also put some ashes under the large tree in Ely Park in Noosaville, a park named after our great old boating mate Len and his family. The tree is known as The Tree of Knowledge, where all the old salts sit and discuss important things.

After the funeral, coming home to a house without an oxygen plant running 24 hours a day, constantly being on hand to tend a sick person, as well as the challenge of living alone for the first time in my life, took a bit of getting used to. It felt quite strange for a while, but one soon becomes used to the changes life throws at you.

It always gives me pleasure to reflect on my husband of nearly 50 years, so here I will briefly recall his life. James Barrie Patrick (*born in the front bedroom at 20 Pommer Street, Brassall* as he was fond of saying), came into the world on May 21, 1934. Barrie, also known to many as Bungee or Bazza, had a mercurial personality, which perhaps explains his entrepreneurial ability and flair for the gimmick. At 16 when we were introduced, I'd never come across this type of person before in my life. Indeed, his whole family was different from my experience of the human race up to this time, and I lacked in the self-confidence department by comparison – my life on the farm was a very sheltered one. He was always seeking new fields and had the desire to depart from the stereotypical "Townie" lifestyle he was born into. Perhaps his time on the Radford farm engendered in him the desire to change his lifestyle.

It was a big step to leave the city behind and head bush (albeit with a young wife, an ex-farm girl). Barrie gained a huge amount of experience from that change of lifestyle on Culladar, which largely completed the change from Townie to Bushie. No doubt his boss, Don Clark-Dickson, played a large part in the transformation. Some of Barrie's jobs during his lifetime were Apprentice Draughtsman with Forrers' (Engineering) in Ipswich, Clerk at the *Queensland Times*, Head Storeman at Woolworths, Pie Cart Owner-Operator, Herd Recorder, Publican and Club Manager, Doorman, Labourer, Ringer and Stock Inspector. A fairly varied career. He'd sold *HOT PIES!*, scraped out locomotive soot, ridden bucking broncs and ran a bush pub when he could have stayed a suburban man. I believe Barrie would have made an exceptional journalist and writer, just like his father. Before he became ill, Barrie did a lot of writing. It's a shame he didn't live long enough to finish the book he'd started to write.

Barrie was also very proud of his Scottish blood – the Lamont Clan (way back). He wore a tie of that tartan and proudly said the Lamonts were notorious Poddy-Dodgers, which seemed strange for a Stock Inspector who was definitely against poddy-dodging. He was proud of Lamont souvenirs brought home for him by various overseas travellers in the family. He claimed to have Scandinavian and Irish blood in his veins also.

Among the numerous articles published in the old days, I will quote here a couple that I think are quite humorous and show the entrepreneurial side of Bazza, the Bastard from the Bush.

After spending a night at The Blue Heeler, one chap wrote that Barrie was: *A tough ex-cattle inspector with a face like a hawk and a mouth like a bear trap.* Another reported: *Barrie Patrick is not your average silken-toned, carefully groomed, nightclub personality. In fact it would be hard to find a man in Australia whose tones are less silky or whose grooming is less careful.*

He probably saw Barrie in his awful wig and Jacky Howe singlet. Quite the contrary, Barrie was pedantic about his personal appearance, but as a showman, he was dedicated to portraying an image, and knew what his audience wanted to see.

He continued: *Barrie has a voice like a chainsaw and the appearance of a man who has never looked in a mirror. But this weekend as if by magic, the grizzled publican of Queensland's most bizarre outback pub will suddenly become a celebrity under lights at Tasmania's exclusive Wrest Point Casino.*

In the years leading up to Barrie's death, Duncan was working in Canada as a helicopter pilot during the Canadian summers, and working back in Australia during our summers, often fighting fires. He initially did his apprenticeship as a mechanical fitter, and had worked hard to become a helicopter pilot. It had been an expensive ambition, the cost of which he toiled for years to meet mostly by working as a marine diesel engineer on prawn vessels.

Deb and Graeme, their children, Harry and Bronte, and Tina once went to Canada on holidays to see Duncan. They were all on board ready for a flight when Tina realised that my whole family was in the one machine. She said, "If we have a fatal crash, Mum will be left on her own". She decided to give the joyride a miss.

Barrie with the two Noels at his 60th birthday party.

Barrie and Harry fishing at Noosaville.

CHAPTER 23

Count Your Blessings

Monday January 13, 2003 seemed like any other Monday during school holidays in my little piece of paradise near Ipswich. Graeme had taken Harry and some friends to the Warrego Water Park, and Deb had taken Bronte (and horses) to the West Moreton Anglican College's Equestrian School. As a mature-age student, Deb obtained two degrees, primary teaching, and speech and drama, and spent some time in the teaching profession after she became a mother, a very good one too. I was having a nana nap after lunch, lying on the bed on the cool side of the house, armed with a novel, with the radio on the bedside table. In between reading and listening to the cricket intermittently, I felt sad. It was two months since we lost Barrie and I felt compelled to play the music that was played at his funeral service. I still felt a bit lost and was inclined to listen out for Barrie calling me and thinking I must check that the oxygen plant in the hallway is working – before I remembered that I didn't need to do that any more. It had become second nature to be on the alert, and in fact when I went to town I always rushed home in case the power had gone off, or Barrie had taken a bad turn. That Monday I was reading Bryce Courtenay's historical novel *Jessica*. It too was reducing me to tears.

At one of my teary moments, at 2.15p.m. to be precise, the phone rang. It was Candace from Heli-Aust in Sydney to tell me Duncan had had an accident in his helicopter.

"Was there a fire?"

"Yes, he was fighting fires in Canberra," she replied.

"No," I said. "Did he get burnt?" It was always a worry for pilots.

"No, he landed in a dam," she said. "He's been taken to the Canberra Hospital. I'll ring back soon."

Normally I would have heard something on the ABC myself, but the cricket broadcast had changed the news breaks. I got off the phone and went berserk. "No! No!" I shouted. I fell to my knees, crying and shocked beyond being sensible. Then I settled down and, all fingers and thumbs, tried to ring Deb. Her phone was on silent and she didn't respond, because the teenagers she was with had been mucking about with it.

I frantically tried Graeme. He was just leaving the Water Park and said he'd go straight to Deb. Earlier, Harry heard about a helicopter accident in Canberra on the car radio and said to his father, "Grandma had a phone call from Duncan in Canberra last night", as if intuitively sensing that it was Duncan in the accident. Before Graeme reached Deb she saw my missed calls and rang me.

Deb reached me quickly, just as Candace from Heli-Aust phoned again. "How soon can you get to Canberra?" she asked.

"We're an hour's drive from the Brisbane Airport. My daughter, Deb, will come with me."

Candace booked two seats on a flight that afternoon. Harry was only 13 at the time and showed maturity beyond his years by ringing Sky Parking near the Brisbane Airport and booking Deb's car in. Packing and getting to the airport was a frantic rush, slowed by my befuddled mind. What to take? How long will I be away? Don't forget your medication, etc. etc. Harry stayed with me while I got ready and his steady presence helped no end. A great lad, Harry, and Graeme did not hesitate to endorse Deb's decision to go with me.

Tina and a friend met us at the parking lot and drove us on to the airport.

During the flight I thought, "I just *can't* lose another of the men in my life". Steven's death was always a sadness just below the surface and Barrie's passing was still very raw. We arrived in Canberra at 8.50pm.

By now we had learnt that Duncan's condition was critical and he required a brain operation as a result of a blow to the head during the accident. Deb's support in Canberra would prove priceless. It would have been hard to cope on my own, such was my state of apprehension and fear. Jim Norrie from Heli-Aust met us at the Canberra Airport and was able to tell us that Duncan was alive, but in a critical condition.

Jim took us to the Heritage Hotel. We booked in, left our luggage there, and continued on to the hospital. Arriving there we went straight to the Intensive Care Ward and were met by a lovely nurse called Sam who gave us details of Duncan's injuries and said the sight of him might shock us. I was pleasantly surprised and relieved as I could only see his left side and could not see much difference, except for all the wires and tubes, and the neck brace in place. However, on walking to his right side I could see where they'd operated to relieve pressure on the brain. There was a great row of staples, a big black eye, and swelling that increased in the days to come.

The staff insisted that we stay at the hospital that first night so Jim went back to the hotel for our luggage and we were taken by a security guard to the hospital accommodation at about 1.45a.m.

Next morning began a long vigil at Duncan's bedside in Intensive Care – a very trying state of affairs, and my heart goes out to anyone in a similar situation. We went back to the hotel at night to have a few hours' sleep, which was hard to achieve, and spent all day and much of the night in the ward, or the waiting room drinking coffee and talking to families in a similar position. The hire car we'd picked up on the first morning meant we could go back and forth independently, as the helicopter pilots who would have helped in that regard were all back on stand-by or fighting the fires, which became worse. The pilots are a very staunch, tight bunch and made sure we were coping, doing all they could to help us.

Meanwhile, Tina flew to Canberra, as did Roger, Duncan's old mate from their school days. On 18th January we went to a shopping centre to get some gear for Duncan, and a few necessities for ourselves. When we went back to the rooftop car park from inside the centre about 3.30pm we were amazed at the sight that met us. It was like night – everything blacked out, with sparks flying through the air – bits of grass on fire. We would later learn that the worst of the fires hit that day when a huge firestorm hit the suburbs of Duffy, Chapman and Holder. Four hundred houses were destroyed and at least four people killed. We weren't the only family in Canberra to be deeply troubled that day. It looked bad to us, and I thought we should get back to the hotel. We had to get fuel for the car first and it was quite a job to find a servo, but we were eventually successful and filled up. We'd later learn that a service station would burn down that night. On the way to the hotel we saw hundreds of people queued up with cats, dogs, birds, etc. waiting to get into emergency centres. They had been evacuated from their homes in the face of the fires.

I made a feeble joke to relieve the tension, "See. As soon as Duncan goes out of action, the fires have got out of control".

By now it was possible to piece the details of the accident together. Duncan was flying his Jet Ranger and picking up water from Bendora Dam in conjunction with three other helicopters. One machine, owned by Snowy Hydro Southcare, and piloted by Mike Toms with crewman Euen McKenzie on board, had been shadowing Duncan since 6.30am as they water-bombed fires in the Namadgi National Park. Around lunchtime, Mike Toms said, "Where's Firebird 248?"

On coming around the side of a hill near the dam they saw the awful truth. Duncan's Jet Ranger was upside down and sinking. The Southcare Helicopter hovered over the machine and Euen jumped in. As he dived down, he saw the door was off and Duncan was hanging upside down, still strapped in. Euen cut him loose and brought him to the surface. He started resuscitation across the upturned helicopter, but it quickly sank so he started for the shore. Jon Stanhope, the ACT's Chief Minister, and Emergency Services director Peter Lucas-Smith, happened to be at the dam and they stripped to their undies to help in the rescue.

Duncan's flying clothes were saturated so the extra manpower helped get the heavy patient to safety. The men then worked to revive Duncan, with the help of Matt O'Brien, a fellow pilot who was working in the area. To their relief, after 20 minutes he started to breathe again.

Matt then took him to the Canberra Hospital in his helicopter where he was operated on for an Extra Dural Haematoma. If Mike Toms had been a couple of minutes later in looking for Duncan, "Firebird 248" would have sunk, and it would have taken quite a while to be found. That would have been a fatal outcome.

There were a number of film crews inspecting the fires that day observing and filming what would become known as the January 2003 Canberra Bushfires. When finally extinguished the damage would reveal: several deaths, over 490 injured, and severe damage to the outskirts of Canberra, the Australian capital city. In one film you can see Duncan take his first breath and one of his mates pats the other on the shoulder as if to say, "We've got him, well done". (It makes me teary to watch. I often wonder how I would have behaved if I had been there on the scene of the rescue – a wreck, I imagine.) Euen McKenzie, who administered CPR, said later that Matt O'Brien was a good calming influence. He kept talking, saying, "Keep breathing, mate, keep breathing". They were determined not to give up.

We didn't actually know what had happened for a while but the newspapers and television were full of the rescue news. Jon Stanhope in his position as ACT's Chief Minister brought a lot of attention to the accident and he, Euen and the pilots involved met us at the hospital and filled us in on the details.

Duncan finally showed some signs of life one day when he opened his eyes and squeezed our hands. We breathed a great sigh of relief and felt sure that he would live. The neck brace came off after a couple of days as the injuries were to the head and a dislocated right shoulder. About a week after the accident, doctors had to take Duncan back to theatre as they were having trouble removing the brain monitor and he required another operation.

While in the Neuro-Acute Ward, Duncan had a couple of falls from a chair and had to be tied to the bed with straps. He hit his head on a rubbish bin and knocked his already dislocated shoulder. While Duncan was in this ward, two men from the "Powers that Be" came to interview him. I don't know whether it was CASA or another section of the hierarchy in the world of aviation such as the Australian Transport Safety Bureau. Duncan was still in a state of confusion. How they expected him to give lucid answers during that 45 minute interview I'll never know.

There was a lot of sadness around the hospital. There were shocking accident cases and sad families everywhere, some enduring far less happy outcomes than ours. The Intensive Care staff were kind and efficient and a great help to relatives.

After a couple of weeks Duncan went into the next ward, the Neuro-Acute ward, the next rung of the ladder in his recuperation. At one stage he said, "Sorry to be such a mungery old bugger". They were his first words on regaining consciousness. On the 10th anniversary of the accident, Duncan, speaking to the press, said that when he opened his eyes and saw he was in hospital he thought "What the hell am I doing in here?"

Deb had to return home and my sister, Barbara, arrived to give me moral and other support. My blood pressure was going through the roof, but Barb was a calming influence. After a couple of weeks in the Neuro-Acute ward, the Air Ambulance flew Duncan to the Princess Alexandra Brain Injury Rehab Unit (BIRU) in Brisbane. Barb and I flew back to Brisbane the same day as Duncan, with Jim Norrie helping us to the Canberra airport.

Duncan beat us to the PA. Attached to his stretcher were the balloons that visitors had brought to him in hospital in Canberra. During his hospitalisation he received dozens of "Get Well" cards and phone calls from across the world, it being such a widely publicised accident and Duncan so well travelled.

All Duncan's gear – his papers, books and personal belongings in his backpack – aboard that ill-fated flight was ruined after a spell underwater. Once the helicopter was reclaimed from the dam it took days to dry everything out, but he never recovered his mobile phone. However, the mention of Jon Stanhope in the Telstra office in Canberra opened a few doors, and Duncan soon had another phone, with the same number. Jon had offered to do anything he could to help after the accident. Sometimes, knowing someone can open a few doors, closed to most of us. The police in Canberra, Federal and local, were of great assistance to us during this time and, among other things, arranged for Tina to get Duncan's car out of the long-term car park in Brisbane, the paperwork having been destroyed in the crash.

Duncan left BIRU about two months after the accident. He had to wait three years to renew his Aviation Medical Certificate and resume flying commercially, although after two years he was permitted to fly on a Class Two Private (Non-commercial) medical certificate. Since the accident, he has undertaken flying jobs all over Australia and also worked in Canada. At the time of writing, he's still going strong and flying in Papua New Guinea.

Once it was all over, we recalled a humorous side to Duncan's rescue. There was a boat stationed at the dam on hand in case of accidents. It was equipped with paramedics and oxygen and when it was on its way to rescue Duncan, the motor on the boat stalled. Those on board started to row to where Duncan was lying on the bank being tended to by his mates. Upon seeing the rescue boat's predicament, one of the airborne helicopter pilots got behind them to blow them ashore, using the downdraught of the rotors.

The terrible days of his accident are never far from mind. I realise how close I was to losing my second son. I'm thankful he has gone on to lead a very busy, some say exciting, life. I am also very proud of how he has returned to a normal and successful life following that terrible accident.

Duncan's flying visit to the Blue Heeler.

Tina's graduation.

CHAPTER 24

The Red Suitcase

One day, Deb came in with a large red suitcase and said, "Mum, now you must travel".

Tina had gone back to school and was studying Journalism at Queensland University when she was awarded a scholarship to City University, London. In 2004 she offered to take her old mum on a holiday in Europe before she started her scholarship. We did a great "European Whirl" coach tour and when Tina began her studies back in London, I went off on a British Isles Tour.

The trips were a great adventure for me. I'd always longed to see that part of the world and gave that red suitcase a good workout. Barrie had no desire to leave our shores and was in his element going to Noosaville with his boat. (He'd never had a passport, but was a very good fisherman.)

I must admit that following the stress of the past couple of years, it was a daunting experience to step on to the tourist coach packed with strangers. It wasn't long though before my anxiety was relieved by the new sights and friendships I made along the way.

While in France I amazed Tina with my knowledge of the French language, rusty though it was. "I didn't know you spoke French, Mum," she said, unaware of my knowledge of grammar-school French.

"Your father and I often conversed in French, especially at the dinner table," I told her. She was even more surprised.

I hope I didn't annoy Tina too much on our tour by singing tunes learnt during my musical career, particularly when we were in Paris. These pertained to the town or situation we were in. Luckily she hadn't taken the British Tour, as I found plenty to sing about there, especially in Ireland and Scotland.

Between bus tours, Tina and I hired a car and did some touring. After visiting friends in Chichester we headed for Crewe in Cheshire, Eva Patrick's birthplace. I took several carefully preserved letters written to her mother, Annie, over the years and we easily found the address of the main letterwriter.

We decided to knock on the door to let the resident know why we were taking photos of the house. Ann, the lady in residence, told us that generations of her family had lived in the house for a couple of hundred years. She was in fact Barrie's second cousin. She was a little reluctant to admit us at first but, after looking at the letters written by her forebears, let us in.

I was overwhelmed. To think this was the house where, nearly 100 years earlier, Nana (Annie) and her husband, William Hughes, had lived and gave birth to Eva. (On a later trip to England with Barbara and Tina we visited the Christ Church in Crewe where Annie Crank had walked down the aisle on Christmas Day, 1902. Following a fire it was slightly different, but the windows and altar were the same.)

Ann introduced us to Mary Oultram, another distant relative, who did an amazing job of tracing the Crank-Hughes relatives, and sketching a family tree for us. After visiting the church and being shown around by some church ladies, we had lunch at a little pub near Crewe with some of the English rellies.

I returned to England again in 2005 on the proceeds of the sale of the "tinnie" and then again in 2009, each time accompanied by my wonderful sister, Barbara.

On my visits to England I felt privileged to be able to attend Evensong at Westminster Abbey. I loved England and Europe and even now I'd go back there again given half the chance. On reflection, I am in awe of Barb's guts and determination, as on that last trip she probably was already feeling the effects of the cancer with which she was later diagnosed. Not that she ever complained.

One of my most memorable trips with that red suitcase was back to the West in 2004 with Barb. We caught the train to Longreach and met up with Deb and Tina to travel by car to Kynuna for the Surf Club Carnival, still being held at The Blue Heeler Hotel. In memory of their father, the girls were competitors in the Royal Flying Doctor Service Spirit of Queensland Awards and did the trip to the carnival as a fundraiser. They stopped in Longreach long enough to do an ABC radio interview promoting the occasion. I found enough used Surf Club shirts of Barrie's to kit out our team, albeit shirts of varying colours and print, but all Blue Heeler shirts from times of old. We two "oldies" sold raffle tickets, and made ourselves useful during the weekend. It was great fun and we raised quite a bit of money. It was the second time I had been in Kynuna since 1980.

I also had a trip or two to Julia Creek for the Dirt and Dust festival with Deb, who was competing in the triathlon. Barbara and I also, on a car trip to Charters Towers, visited Rubyvale and Anakie in The Gemfields on the way. Tina's first full-time job as a journalist was at the *Northern Miner* in The Towers and she reconnected with our old drover mate, Tiddley Triffett, and his partner, Olly Daly, who were both very good to her. The West was quite an eye-opener for Barbara and a good opportunity for me to catch up with old friends (and sample some of Tiddley's famous damper, as Barrie had all those years ago in Julia Creek). Barb and I did many trips together as widows with a keen desire to see more of the world, although Barb travelled much more than I. Barbara was a staunch worker and supporter of the Pittsworth Historical Society and after she turned 80 the Museum dedicated a room to her – a fitting recognition of her efforts over many years. I love all my siblings and we still have a strong family bond and meet as often as possible. Sadly we lost Barb on September 9, 2014. She was 83. I still miss her terribly – we really were the best of friends as well as the closest of sisters.

Lori with her niece Janet and sister Kath.

Lori and sister Barbara.

CHAPTER 25

My Home Among the Gum Trees

Now in my 81st year, I often think about the great times I shared with Barrie and the many adversities we faced. We were a top team and I do miss him, but am regularly reminded of the wonderful times we shared. Sitting here in my "home among the gum trees" is comparatively quiet, but there is enough to keep this publican's wife busy.

One of my pleasures is the 60 and Better Choir in Ipswich. This has been a chance to renew my acquaintance with music, a most rewarding experience. The members of the Concert Party are a wonderful group of people, all happy volunteers, and the weekly practice and concerts we perform at nursing homes and retirement villages are very satisfying and enjoyable. Quite a few of our members are older than the people we entertain. There is nothing like music to keep one feeling young. The accordion still gets thrown in when I'm heading off to a family party. I shared the stage again recently with my sister, Kath, and niece, Janet at Kath's 80th. Just like the old times, but with the next generation of Harsants joining in.

The solidarity in the family of Radford and Jessie Harsant remains strong and I think, without exception, we have lived useful and fulfilling lives and stuck together through thick and thin. As I mentioned, we lost Barbara in 2014 and my sister, Miri, also left us in 1994 after a battle with breast cancer. I still remain in regular contact with my sisters, Margaret, Kath and Ann, and brothers, John and Rob and of course all my wonderful nieces and nephews. Dad and Mum were of families of seven, I am one of eight, but I only have two grandchildren, but then most families are much smaller these days. What we lack in quantity, though, is made up for in quality. Joining our strand of the family tree to that of the Patricks has come up trumps! Barrie's brother, Don, passed away in 1994, but we share a lovely relationship with his son, Aaron, who lives and works in Melbourne.

I am very proud of my grandchildren, Harry and Bronte. They have both been to university and are carving out successful careers, sometimes off the beaten track. Bronte, following in her grandma's footsteps, has worked out West. Harry is a successful television personality in China, no doubt possessing the same entertainment gene as Bazza. I am equally proud of Duncan, Deb and Tina and spend a lot of time with them all. I still remember Steven each day.

I keep my mind sharp by filling the positions of Secretary, Treasurer and Chairman of the Body Corporate of our Noosaville unit that we have owned since we left the pub. I quite enjoy the job, not that there is any reward except the satisfaction in being able to keep the books straight and the money honestly spent. The other owners trust me and no-one else wants the job at this stage. I will probably keep accepting the position until I feel it is beyond my capabilities. We have had some great people in our community of owners and a contribution of lovely freshly caught fish is always most welcome.

Well, that's about it – most of my memories used up. Now the writing is finished and out of my system I might have time and inclination to complete a few barely started projects, like learning to play the ukulele Barbara gave me for Christmas in 2012. I'd also like to take in a few shows in Brisbane, opera and ballet perhaps. Mostly though I'd like to wear out that red suitcase!

Life has been pretty good to me. Yes, I have been up a few dry gullies, but I've been fortunate to live the life I have. When my dad was 65 he said, "I think I will live another 15 years, *barring accidents*". He did better than that, I'm glad to say. I hope the same will be true for me – there's still a bit of life in this Old Grey Mare yet.

Harsant siblings later in life.

Lori with her family at Tina & Steve's wedding in March 2015.

Lori.

Singing in The 60 and Better Choir in Ipswich.

Glossary

Billy lids Kids or children

CWA Country Women's Association

Cut a few capers Playing up

Dunger A lowly worker on a station

Gidgee bug A type of insect commonly found in the West

Last Shoe repairing mould

Poddy-dodger A cattle thief

Queensland Salute (slang) The wave people out West give to ward off flies

Semi Semi-trailer

Stockie Stock Inspector working for the Department of Agriculture

The Bush Less populated areas of Australia

The Creek Julia Creek

The Centre Central Australia

The Combo A waterhole near Kynuna

The Curry Cloncurry

The Isa Mount Isa

The Territory Northern Territory (NT)

The Wet The wet season of northern Australia. **Big Wet:** an exceptionally wet period

The West or Out West Used in Queensland for country beyond the populated, eastern area of the State